HAPPY, NOT TORTURED

A Mental Health Guide For Artists and Creative People

By

Céline Terranova

ISBN: 979-8-639-55301-1

Website: theparttimeartist.com
Email: info@theparttimeartist.com

CONTENTS

INTRODUCTION

Welcome, dear Reader. I am so happy to virtually meet you!

My name is Céline Terranova. I'm a writer from Belgium, currently living in London and sometimes working in theatre. You might know me from my podcast, my blog or my first book, that all share the same name: *The Part-Time Artist*. Through all these projects, I have had one goal: to help other creative people live their best life.

With my first book, published in March 2019, I helped artists like you find enough time, energy and motivation to do their art, despite the fact that most of us need to have a job-to-pay-the-bills and therefore have very limited time. I talked about subjects as varied as earning money, searching for a job and starting your own business. And I also talked about mental health.

My idea was to give some pointers developed from what I do to keep myself sane and happy. But since I published, I found that there was much more to the subject that needed to be said. This year, I spoke to plenty of artists, I interviewed a handful of them on the podcast, and I read a lot of accounts about how badly mental health was impacting people's lives. And I decided that I needed to write more about it.

This is how this book was born.

I have had my own struggles with mental health. I've battled depression and self-esteem issues. In December 2017, I was diagnosed with a General Anxiety Disorder (GAD). It took six months of therapy for me to get the hang of how to live with it. I had horrible thoughts and panic attacks, and it was quite a difficult experience to go through. But I came out on the other side and I had to re-learn how to take care of myself without the help of therapy. I went back to some of my old passions that I had given up on in the midst of all the stress, and I developed new supportive habits to help myself.

I still have bad days, of course. On these days, I feel overwhelmed, I feel depressed, I feel like I'm a loser and a mess. I wake up and I know it's going to be a bad day. My anxiety is already through the roof because I slept badly or I had a nightmare. My mood varies from morose to angry for no reason. On days like these, I can't interact with people without feeling terrible or being snappy. I become terrified about anything and everything. All news is bad news. Every thought about the future is full of dread and catastrophe. I find it impossible to concentrate on my goals. These are when I use a lot of distractions to numb the pain or dread or guilt at the idea that I should do something productive. Everything I think is just plainly negative, and no matter what I try, it stays that way.

Therefore, the most important skill I have had to learn is to keep writing even when I have a bad day. I don't think I've ever met a creative person who hasn't struggled with mental health at some point in their career, and for most of them it has impacted their creativity. I've seen some people become so overwhelmed with these issues that they've stopped creating completely.

So, this book is going to be all about creating despite our mental health, the same way that *The Part-Time Artist* was about creating despite having no time for it. I'm going to talk about my experiences, my mistakes, my bad habits and things that helped me along the way. I intend to be completely honest and open about my struggles and my victories, because I think you might identify with some of them.

Mental health is not an easy topic to talk about, but I hope that this book will open the discussion. My strategies and techniques are in no way a finite list of what works and what doesn't. You will have to try and test them, perhaps research more and pick the ones that give the best results.

I am grateful that you have chosen me to accompany you on your journey to better mental health, and I will do my best to be as informative and clear as possible.

IMPORTANT DISCLAIMER

Before we start, it is important to note that this book is mostly about prevention. While there is a chapter about crisis, based on my training and experience as Mental Health First Aider, it will only contain the basics. This book is not a replacement for antidepressants or professional therapy.

My aim is to give you tools to look after yourself and develop good habits that will help you safeguard your own mental health. I am not a therapist or a counsellor. I'm basing this book on my personal experience, training and extensive research.

If you are experiencing severe symptoms, such as suicidal thoughts, I urge you to speak to a professional.

WORKBOOK

Along with this book, I have also prepared a workbook. The idea is that, while you are reading, you can complete the workbook with your own answers. When you finish it, you'll have your personalised strategy that you can read again whenever you need it.

To download the workbook, follow the link:

ThePartTimeArtist.com/Happy-Workbook

MENTAL HEALTH AND CREATIVITY

WHAT IS MENTAL HEALTH?

If you have picked up this book, you might have had "run-ins" with mental illnesses before. Or you might feel like something is not quite right. You might feel constantly anxious or depressed but never had a solid diagnostic. You might feel like your mood is varying beyond what is normally yours, or you might simply be scared that you'll get gradually worse and worse.

No matter what your reasons are, I'm here to tell you that there isn't a strict line between "mental illness" and "mental health". There aren't just "sane" and "insane" people either. Mental health is a spectrum, and you move up and down that spectrum all the time.

Professionals usually define your mental health as good if you can cope with your life, if you feel mostly happy and if you play your part in your family, job and community. As you can see, it's not a very precise definition. A deteriorating mental health means that you feel stressed, overwhelmed, mostly unhappy, that you can't cope with what life throws at you and that you can't fulfil your role in your family, job or community.

The thing is, these feelings can very well be temporary. If you receive several pieces of bad news in a row and find it hard to keep going after that, it doesn't necessarily mean that you need to do anything about your mental health. Very often, these feelings will go away when circumstances change.

But sometimes, circumstances don't change rapidly enough, or your emotional state doesn't go back to what you experienced as "normal", which might indicate that there is something afoot. And sometimes, you can feel your mood starting to change without any exterior explanation.

Mental health is a tricky subject to approach because not only is every experience unique, but there is also a huge stigma associated with it. The recurring theme here is that if you experience these issues, you don't need to "get yourself together", "change your mindset", or even the infamous "man up".

In this chapter, I want to talk about mental health for artists in particular because not only do issues present themselves more frequently for artists, but there doesn't seem to be enough efforts made to improve the situation.

MENTAL HEALTH IN THE CREATIVE INDUSTRIES

According to a study from Ulster University[1], workers in the creative industries are three times more likely to develop a mental health problem than the general population. This is based on a study of 574 people who work in the creative sector. Common issues cited by the participants were anxiety (36%) and depression (32%).

The study found that specific characteristics of the creative sector contributed to the likelihood of developing mental health problems. For example, pressure to reach high standards, irregular work, irregular financial income and the perceived lack of value for the work done were all cited by participants of the study.

This doesn't surprise me at all. I've worked in the theatre industry for the past six years, and I have had my fair share of problems linked to these jobs. These problems definitely contributed to aggravating my stress. In fact, my anxiety became really bad last year due to a very negative work environment. I have lived thought the fear of having a

---

[1] Ulster University and Inspire Wellbeing for All (Author unspecified), "Changing Arts and Minds: A Survey of Health and Wellbeing in the Creative Sector". https:// www.inspirewellbeing.org/media/9241/changing-arts-and-minds-creative-industries-summary.pdf (accessed 26 Feb. 2020)

zero-hour contract and not knowing if I'll be able to pay my rent next month. I've been shouted at, spat at and vomited on at work. I've had to deal with long antisocial hours and lack of relationships outside of the theatre world. The creative industries are especially bad at dealing with these issues, and if you work in such a sector, you are probably facing similar problems.

But the question is: are these mental health problems solely created by the bad working conditions? Or are they already present, lurking in the shadows until these specific circumstances make them appear? In other words, does being creative mean that you are more likely to develop a mental health problem, regardless of your circumstances?

The answer is... maybe. Scientific studies don't all agree on this. One study[2] found that writers specifically are more likely to suffer from schizophrenia, bipolar disorder, unipolar depression, anxiety disorders, substance abuse, and suicidal thoughts. But it is very difficult to separate biology and environment. It's the good old nature vs nurture dilemma: which part is already there, and which part appears later?

Until scientists are able discern exactly how our creative brains function, I think it is fair to assume that we might be more at risk, especially when the circumstances of our work make our lives more difficult.

What does that mean for you personally? It means that, as an artist, you are more likely to encounter issues such as anxiety, depression, suicidal thoughts or panic attacks. Along your career, that could span twenty, forty or even more years, you are likely to either develop such problems yourself or know someone who will.

If this is such an inescapable truth of the life of an artist, how come there is so little help for those of us who suffer from it?

---

[2] Kyaga, Simon et al., "Mental illness, suicide and creativity: 40-Year prospective total population study", *Journal of Psychiatric Research* Vol. 47(1) (2013), pp. 83-90. Available online here: https://www.sciencedirect.com/science/article/abs/pii/S0022395612002804?via%3Dihub (accessed 26 Feb. 2020)

THE TORTURED ARTIST

I've written about this briefly in The Part-Time Artist: as a society, we have an imagined representation of "the Artist" (with a capital A) as a tortured soul, who submits themself to the torment of mental torture for the sake of their art.

I've also said that I hate this notion. I hate it with passion, and not just because it's a stereotype. For many artists, this turns into a self-fulfilling prophecy. You are expected to be tortured, so you torture yourself. And you don't get help. On purpose!

This notion is reinforced every time someone talks about being a "real" something. A "real" writer, a "real" actor, a "real" musician. No matter which field you are in, I bet there is the "right" way to be "it", and that way is probably overly difficult, tortuous and involves a lot of internal screaming. Have you heard the saying, "the most successful people are the most troubled"? Someone told me that one day, and at the time I wasn't as clued in on mental health and thought it was probably true.

In real life, identifying yourself as a tortured artist is self-destructive behaviour. It can mean that you abuse some substances, that you don't seek help and consider mental health problems "good" for you, because they fuel your creativity.

Observe how many artistic geniuses destroyed themselves with drugs, alcohol, medicines or self-harm over the centuries. This is not a new concept. On the contrary, it is a dangerous belief, even more so because even when countless of artists have died, we still romanticise the notion of the tortured artist.

The expectation put on artists to act this way is so ingrained in our society that most people don't see how devastating the effects are. This is a big reason why so many of us struggle with mental health issues for years, even decades, and think it's perfectly normal. This is why employers in the creative industry don't make much efforts to improve the environment of their employees, because it's "normal" to struggle as an artist. And this is also why we hear about so many talented artists, sometimes extremely successful ones, who take their own life after years and years of suffering.

And yet, we do nothing. Because it's the "artist's life", because it's the rule, because those who came before suffered, so we must suffer too.

To this, I say no. I say that it's time to design mental health programmes specifically adapted for the artistic temperament. It's time that we take care of ourselves and others in the same field. It's time for employers to invest in their employees' wellbeing.

And if you are reading this, I suspect you think, maybe deep deep down, that it's time to do something for yourself too. If that's the case, bear with me.

PREVENTION VS. TREATMENT

Earlier this year, the Guardian ran a series of articles[3] about mental illnesses that are estimated to affect almost a billion people worldwide. They interviewed physicians, experts and mental health specialists who all agreed on one major thing: prevention in mental health is the way to go.

Preventing illnesses instead of treating them is not really a groundbreaking idea. That's what we do with many illnesses. We promote exercise to fight against cardiovascular problems. We use vaccines against many devastating diseases. And we sometimes perform preventive surgeries to reduce the risk of cancer.

Prevention is a the heart of modern medicine, but it is different when it comes to mental health. Often, prevention is not mentioned unless you get a specific diagnosis. Of course, prevention in mental health is tricky, because mental illnesses can come from different factors: environment, genetics, certain events and other mechanisms that haven't yet been identified.

Who is responsible for these factors? Certainly, a good healthcare system should be able to screen for some genetically recurring illnesses. It would also be beneficial to include psychological assessments or screening in schools, to detect abuse and other issues early in childhood. In some countries, these mechanisms are already in place. But you and I know full well that it's not the case everywhere, and that existing measures are usually not enough.

So, should we completely abandon prevention? Not at all! On the contrary, I strongly believe that methods to promote a good mental health should be taught in schools, and in particular, in artistic schools. I believe that if we are better informed and trained in some techniques, we can all fare much better in our lives and careers, and cope with a lot of the things that will happen along the way.

---

[3] Various Authors, "In Mind: Focus on Mental Health", The Guardian: https://www.theguardian.com/society/series/in-mind-focus-on-mental-health (accessed 26 Feb. 2020)

In the next chapters, we are going to observe behaviours and aggravating factors that can make your mental health worse. Then, we will work on why we display these behaviours in the first place, and how we can replace them with more productive habits.

Prevention is, before anything, something you can do without anyone else's involvement. It can make the difference between having a tough time and going into a deep depression. It can help turn a severe anxiety problem into a milder version of it. It can also help you to help other people. If you know what to do, you can advise someone who is having a hard time, recognise symptoms and suggest changes that could help them.

The more people who are educated in mental health, the more we will be able to fight these illnesses. Herd immunity is not just for vaccines!

YOUR OLD MENTAL HEALTH DIET

Bad Habits Mean Bad Results

In this chapter, I will spend some time observing and describing the habits that make our mental health worse. In other words, the "diet" that a lot of us are following.

There are many indicators of a bad mental health diet, and it is very likely that you are not going to have all the behaviours that I'm going to talk about. But it is probable that you indulge in some of them, perhaps quite often.

For now, I only want you to notice these behaviours in yourself. You can use the workbook to follow the sections of this chapter and write down when something corresponds to you.

This is an important work, "noticing". Being aware of what you do and think is an extremely powerful tool to improve your life. It doesn't mean that you need to beat yourself up because you do some (or many) of these things. Be fair with yourself and recognise that most of these habits are completely subconscious, which means that, until someone points them out to you, they are almost impossible to pinpoint.

So, for now, let's just notice and not judge.

Bad Brain Diet

"Nothing travels faster than the speed of light, with the possible exception of bad news, which obeys its own special laws."
– Douglas Adams

The first obvious habit that I'm going to talk about is what you put into your brain. Everything that you watch, listen to and read, everything that you absorb from the world around you.

All this information comes in three different flavours: positive, negative and neutral, depending on how they make you feel when you receive them. For example, reading a blog post with advice and encouragement is likely to motivate you. Therefore, it goes in the "positive" category. Another example is an article on a news website that talks about a terrible accident in great detail. It is likely to make you feel sad, depressed or horrified. That goes in the "negative" category. And the neutral category is for everything that doesn't particularly influence your emotions, such as a TV show that you watch distractedly to pass the time.

Now, observe these categories, particularly the negative and the positive. Is one of them bigger than the other? If you are anything like me, you probably have much more stuff in the negative bin than the positive one. As we get up in the morning, we are immediately assailed with bad news, from social media to news media.

And this is not surprising. Our society is rigged to show us the worst of humanity repeatedly, especially with how the internet has made the access to this information far easier and tailored to us. Have you watched a news programme lately? It will be full of the worst dramas in politics, the worst events in crime and the worst predictions for the future.

As human beings, we are also attracted to it, let's not deny it. I sometimes find myself reading terrible stories on Reddit about people I've never met, and these stories often make me feel terrible. But I keep on reading. Why? I'm not sure. It's like a voyeuristic instinct, the same kind that makes people slow down near a car crash. It's what makes us feverishly read news stories about celebrities, the trashier the better. Media groups have understood this very well and make millions from our lack of restraint when it comes to wanting more gory details.

What are the consequences of this assault of negativity from the outside? Similar to eating junk food, feeding your mind with crap won't make much of a difference if you only do it for one day. But do it consistently over a long period of time, and you are likely to create lasting problems such as low mood, hopelessness, anxiety or depression.

Habits Checklist: Do you spend hours ingesting content that makes your feel unhappy, angry or depressed? Do you open a news app as soon as you wake up in the morning? Do you watch the news several times a day? Do you keep yourself up to date on the latest celebrity scandal? How full is your "negative" bin on a day to day basis?

RUMINATION

"If you realised just how powerful your thoughts are, you would never think a negative thought."
– Peace Pilgrim

As you probably know, you don't need to receive negative information from the outside to have negative thoughts. Our heads are full of them, and even if you don't feed them, they thrive and swim freely in your mind. I'm convinced that, even if I only received positive news in a day, my brain could easily turn everything into negative. It's sort of a superpower. A dumb superpower.

This is called rumination: dwelling on negative thoughts exaggeratedly. It means thinking constantly about rejection, loss, failure and stress, even if they happened a long time ago. It also means thinking in absolutes, such as, "I'm always this", "they never do that". Generalisations are also negative thoughts.

Think of your mind as a pub. You have the regulars, the people that are there often enough to be recognised by the serving team, and then the other patrons, the passersby, the people who come once in a while, maybe even just one time. The thoughts you entertain the most in your mind are the regulars, and the serving team (your brain) knows exactly how to react to them. So if these thoughts are constantly negative, your brain will become used to the negativity and make it easier and easier for those regular thoughts to come back. Even if a positive "customer" adventures inside the mind, it will feel out of place, awkward and leave quickly.

Habits Checklist: Think about your own mind. Who are the regular customers? Who is always there, hanging at the bar, waiting to share their opinion? Who comes back, over and over, knowing full well they'll find a place to thrive? Noticing rumination can be tricky, as most of the time we don't realise the exact thoughts we think about. You might need a few days to do this work.

GRUDGES

"To be wronged is nothing unless you continue to remember it."
– Confucius

We've seen that allowing negative thoughts to thrive in your brain will more than likely alter your mood. But there's a specific type of negative thought that is going to make even more damage: grudges

Let me tell you the story of my previous employment. I used to be a manager in charge of a team of forty people. I carried out recruitment, training, health and safety assessments, and duty managed several nights a week, amongst many other responsibilities. It was stressful and overwhelming, but I know I could have done a good job if it weren't for my bosses. They methodically destroyed every shred of confidence I had, making me believe that I was doing an awful job, saying that if I wasn't there, it wouldn't make a difference for the company, pushing me to break and resign.

I have such a hard time letting this story go, even though it's been over a year now since I left. When someone attacks the core of who you are, it's difficult to get over it. I still fantasise about revenge in my head. I still have nightmares about that job. It's not over, and I don't know how to let it go. This has a very bad influence on my mood and mental health.

Grudges are amongst the most difficult thoughts to suppress. They permeate everything we do and every thought we think, and they don't disappear. On the contrary, they can last for years if you are not careful. And the thing is, we don't always want to get rid of them. We feel like we are in the right, and the other party was in the wrong. So why would we let them go?

Habits Checklist: Do you have a grudge, a past event or simply a resentment that, whatever you do, you can't let go of? Do you find that there is someone that you simply can't forgive, no matter how much time has passed? And how does it make you feel when you think about it?

FESTERING LONELINESS

"We are all so much together, but we are all dying of loneliness."
– Albert Schweitzer

I've talked about negative thoughts and information, but now I'm going to talk about a nourishing soil that will make those grow and fester your brain much quicker than any compost: loneliness.

Loneliness doesn't necessarily mean that you are alone all day long and don't speak to any living soul for weeks. Although, for some people, this is exactly the case. But for most, loneliness can happen even if you are surrounded by people all the time.

When I worked at my previous job, I was around other people all day. I had colleagues, customers and staff members, and yet I felt terribly lonely. I didn't like the job; I hated the environment and I felt like I couldn't confide in anyone. I also thought that, if I tried to explain to anyone how I felt, they wouldn't understand. The fact that I was working unsociable hours, and therefore only socialised with people from work made me feel even more isolated.

I feel like I've been lonely many times in my life, and it's a disease that I can't seem to completely shake off. I felt terribly lonely when I was a teenager and dreamt of science fiction, books and magic, while nobody else seemed to understand. I felt lonely when I studied physics and hated every second of it, while everyone around me seemed so passionate about the field. I never felt lonelier than when I moved to Switzerland to do a PhD, knowing nobody there, and couldn't find any help when my then boss started to bully me. I felt lonely again when I was depressed and aimless, with no end to the suffering in sight.

If I could choose to end one thing in this world, it would be loneliness. I believe that if we could find a way to be more connected to each other, to talk, to feel understood, a lot of mental health problems would disappear. Unfortunately, such a mechanism doesn't exist. The internet has made some interactions easier because you can keep contact with people living in different countries. You can always find a community of strangers who share your interest somewhere, no matter how niche that interest is. But online connections are not the same as human interactions. And the internet can make us feel more lonely because now we can see other people connecting, other people having fun, without us.

Loneliness compounds negative thoughts. Without anyone to confide in or to straighten us up, our brains turn into echo chambers, forever repeating the same thoughts over and over again, getting darker and darker.

Habits Checklist: Do you feel lonely? Is it a constant feeling, or does it pass? Right now, if you had a really bad day, could you call someone and talk about it? Or are you scared of bothering them? Can you confide in the people around you?

COMPARISON

> *"Comparison is the thief of joy."*
> *– Theodore Roosevelt*

I've talked about spying on other people's social media profiles and feeling excluded from their events and parties, but there's another side effect to this behaviour: comparison.

When I hear about a new author who wrote the new "sensation" in science fiction or self-help, my first reaction is always to see how old they are. It's almost unconscious. My goal is to see if that person is older or younger than me. Older? Then it's fine; I can still aim at becoming as successful as them. Younger? Then I'm a loser, or they were well-connected, depending on the level of pettiness I feel at the time.

I even do it with my entertainment—I compare my unfinished first draft of a novel to a popular series or bestseller book, and of course, the result is that I'm demoralised because I feel that mine is not as good. Comparison creeps up in every aspect of life, not just the artistic. I compare myself to people I see on Facebook, particularly people my age who have achieved (as I perceive it) more than I have. They own a house and I still rent a small flat. They have kids while I'm not even married. They have a car and go on holiday, while I can't afford any of these things.

The troubling thing about comparison is that we often use it to put ourselves down. I find it very rare that I compare myself to someone that I perceive as "less" than me. Most of my comparisons end the same way: I'm not good enough.

Comparison is so ingrained in ourselves because we have been shown how to do it since childhood. I remember hearing my parents comparing my grades to those of other children in primary school. I remember them showing me other children as an example of what to do, how to be, who to follow, to be more of this or less of that.

Now, as an adult and an artist, I see comparison everywhere. Newcomers are compared to their predecessors, fans compare new work with old ones and artists themselves can't help but look around and see how they fare compared to others in the difficult creative industry. We can't escape it.

Habits Checklist: How often do you compare yourself to other people? Do you try to be objective, giving yourself a break, or do you use other people to beat yourself up? How does someone else's success make you feel?

PERFECTIONISM

"Insecurity's best cover is perfectionism. That's where it becomes an art form."
– Beth Moore

Another behaviour that is often favoured by artists is perfectionism. Am I the only one who scowls at a typo found in a book, even if it's the only one in the eighty thousand words that I have read? Am I the only one who delays the release of a project so that I can check one more time that everything is fine? I don't think so.

My perfectionism is born out of anxiety. Trying to get everything perfect is a way for me to control an uncontrollable outcome. If I double and triple-check this book, it can't fail, right? I can't get negative reviews if I've made sure every single paragraph is as flawless as possible. Of course, that's not how it works, but it appeases my anxious thoughts for a little while, so it feels worth it. Even if it means being awake at 4.00 a.m., changing all the headings of my book to a different font.

The problem with being perfect is that we are human, and therefore not perfect. It means setting standards that are impossible to reach, even if we try hard. I can't count the number of times I've been disappointed with myself because the words that fell on the page didn't look nearly as good as the ones in my head. As I'm writing this book, I am already thinking that it will go through a lot of revisions, because I don't like what I've written so far.

Honestly, perfectionism feels like torture sometimes. These thoughts never leave you, and they make every success feel "less than". Recently, I've found some typos in The Part-Time Artist. I've also had an author that I admire buy the book just before I could correct the typos. I had to stop myself from sending them a message with the new, typo-free version. This incident stopped me from promoting my book for a whole week!

I know these thought processes come from my childhood, in part because I had parents who were quick to point out the one fault in an otherwise pretty good performance. They are the type of people who, when I got a 99% grade, asked why I didn't get the last percent. I know that it was not malicious at all—it was just their way of instilling in me a hunger for success. But as many children of perfectionist parents know, it took away the pleasure of accomplishment. Sometimes I wish I had just been told "good job", and nothing more.

Habits Checklist: Do you have the same unhealthy aim of perfection as me? Do you think about the one small mistake you made when someone compliments you on an achievement? How much does it impact your life?

SELF-DOUBT

"Whether you believe you can do a thing or not, you are right."
– Henry Ford

While doubting yourself is not always bad (for example, if you think you can jump on the back of a bear, better question yourself!), the repetition of self-doubt is another destructive habit to watch out for.

Self-doubt becomes unhealthy when it is chronic. It comes in the form of unhelpful affirmations that come to your mind over and over when you attempt something, such as, "I can't, I shouldn't, I'm not—"

When repeated often enough, self-doubt builds an impenetrable barrier in your mind that limits you more and more. Do you want to hear my biggest self-doubt thought? "I can't maintain a routine for a long period of time." It comes from childhood, when I would start something, get super into it, then get bored and give up. Every time, I would be frustrated that I couldn't stick with anything.

I carried this belief about myself into adulthood, and it has become a self-fulfilling prophecy. I start plenty of things, then get bored and move on, but carry the shame and guilt that I didn't continue. I've done it with things as varied as hobbies, jobs, diets and gyms. All were started with a lot of enthusiasm and abandoned within a couple of months. Frankly, the only thing I've ever stuck with has been writing, and I sometimes even doubt that I can stick with that much longer.

It's difficult to try new things, to be adventurous and be bold when you have the belief that you can't do it. It makes being an artist very difficult too. I catch myself thinking that I can't do something when, realistically, if I gave it a try, I might be able to do it. I just don't try, because "it's not me".

Habits Checklist: Do you constantly question your abilities, or whether you can really do what you dream of? Do you give up before even starting because you are sure that you won't succeed? Do you trust yourself? Do you often wonder if you made the right decision, or if you can do a thing at all? What has it cost you?

UNHEALTHY LIFESTYLE

"Take care of your body. It's the only place you have to live."
– Jim Rohn

I am the first to appreciate a good glass of wine from time to time, to sleep less than the recommended number of hours, or to get a big McDonalds order in when I feel like it. Indulging in unhealthy habits is fun, it's comforting and it feels good sometimes to be bad.

But I've also noticed that, immediately after indulging, I get a backlash in my mood. Alcohol, in particular, is bad for my anxiety. If I drink more than a glass, the next day I feel depressed and overwhelmed by everything. It scares me and makes me uneasy too because I have a family history of alcoholism. There were times in my life when I drank almost every day, when I felt the lowest and the most lost. Alcohol only made me feel better for a little while. The next day, usually, it was worse.

Without even talking about addiction, substances and behaviours that are bad for your body are often bad for your mind, too. Junk foods make your brain produce endorphins, but also induce a "lack" after a while, which can make you more depressed than before.

Sleep deprivation is another huge factor in mental health problems. If you don't sleep enough, you don't get enough REM sleep (deep sleep), which normally helps you process events and emotions. Insomnia is closely associated with depression, whether causing it, making it worse or triggering an underlying mental health problem. I suffer from insomnia, and I know that when I've only had a couple of hours' of sleep, I feel less optimistic, more morose and also more anxious. Even without insomnia, I've noticed that if I sleep less, my anxiety gets worse.

Habits Checklist: If you had to judge from the outside, how healthy is your lifestyle? Do you indulge more often than not? Do you sleep enough? How is it impacting on your mental health?

INACTIVITY

"The vast majority of buttocks are overused, whereas that of minds are underused."
— Mokokoma Mokhonoana

One of the side effects of quitting my job in January 2019 was that I suddenly saw my level of activity decrease drastically. Before quitting, I was going to work six days a week, I was commuting, I was walking, I was going up and down the stairs a lot. Post-quitting, my only physical activity was to walk between my bedroom and my desk.

I've never been one for exercising regularly. I hate going to the gym, I hate running, and most exercise classes either bore me or make my back problems worse. But I noticed, over the months after I quit my job, that the lack of physical activity had severe consequences on my mental health.

The first consequence was that I gained weight. It didn't concern me too much until I could not fit into most of my clothes, which caused my self-esteem to crumble.

The second, and most pernicious consequence, was that my brain didn't produce the precious endorphins that I needed to feel good about myself. Whether I want it or not, exercising produces endorphins that make me happy. Without them, there was just negativity and depression.

It is proven[4] that inactivity will increase depressive symptoms. Studies have shown that people who stop exercising experience an impact on their mental health almost immediately. This is even more pronounced in women than men.

Habits Checklist: What is your level of physical activity? Do you only walk between your bed and your desk, too? Do you sit all day long? Do you skip your workouts regularly?

CLUTTER

"Visible mess helps distract us from the true source of the disorder."
– Marie Kondō

One of the first symptoms that appear when my mental health degrades is the chaos in my flat. When my mind feels cluttered, so do my living quarters. The thing is, clutter begets clutter. Soon enough, clutter becomes the thing that causes anxiety. It's a vicious circle.

The problem is that I hate cleaning and tidying. They feel (rightly) like chores, and like a big waste of time. Cleaning my flat means that it uses time that could be spent writing, and some days chores feel extremely pointless. Why do the dishes when tomorrow there will be another pile? Why do laundry when more clothes will be used and will need to be cleaned? What gets me about chores is that they are never done once and for all. That means that there are ups and downs in how tidy and clean everything around me is, and my mental health correspondingly goes up and down with it.

Living in a cluttered environment can cause anxiety in itself. If you're anything like me, every time you see clutter, it might make you feel guilty, anxious, overwhelmed or all of the above. In the same way that a cluttered desk can be distracting and reduce productivity, a cluttered

---

[4] Morgan, Julie A. et al., "Does ceasing exercise induce depressive symptoms? A systematic review of experimental trials including immunological and neurogenic markers", *Journal of Affective Disorders* vol. 234 (2018) pp. 180-192. Available online here: https://www.sciencedirect.com/science/article/abs/pii/S0165032717317494 (accessed 27 Feb. 2020)

home can lead you to concentrate on unimportant things.

Clutter is a type of overstimulation that can really take a toll on your mind, especially if you already have issues focusing. Anxiety, depression and cluttering feed each other and turn into a vicious circle. When I feel too depressed to tidy up, I feel guilty because my flat is dirty, and the guilt feeds depressive feelings. It doesn't end.

Habits Checklist: Look around you. Is you home relatively tidy? We all have busy lives, and a little bit of mess is not the end of the world, but where do you tend to stand on the spectrum between tidiness and chaos? Does clutter make you feel guilty, sad or morose?

BOTTLING UP

"Unexpressed emotions will never die. They are buried alive and will come forth later in uglier ways."
– Sigmund Freud

To be a functioning adult, we all had to learn to control our emotions. We can't all explode at the slightest irritation (although I've worked in customer service long enough to know that some people *do* explode when displeased, but they are fortunately the minority).

Since childhood, you have probably been taught to control yourself, to not make a scene, to process your emotions in a milder way. In particular, if you are a man you might have been taught to repress sadness, and if you are a woman you might have been pushed to repress anger. The degree of the repression depends strongly on your upbringing and culture, but we've all had to do it one way or another.

But repressing emotions is pernicious, and soon enough we find ourselves repressing things that should not be repressed at all. The problem is that many of us confuse bottling up emotions with dealing with them. Pushing an emotion, which is a natural response to an event, deep deep down is not a way to deal with it. Ideally, it should only be repressed temporarily, until you know what do to with it, but this is often not what happens.

Studies[5] have shown that the mechanism of regulating emotions is an essential feature of mental health, and when it becomes dysfunctional, that's when problems start. In fact, bottling up emotions does not only

---

[5] Gross, James J. and Ricardo F. Muñoz, "Emotion Regulation and Mental Health", *Clinical Psychology: Science and Practice*, vol. 2(2) (1995), pp. 151-164. Available online here: https://onlinelibrary.wiley.com/doi/full/10.1111/j.1468-2850.1995.tb00036.x (accessed 27 Feb. 2020)

cause mental health issues, but studies[6] have also shown a very strong link between repression and severe physical health conditions such as cancer.

So, in all that, where you do you lie? I'm a pro at concealing and bottling up my emotions. Up until I was twenty-five years old, I did not speak up for myself nearly as much as I do now, which I'm sure created depression after years of abuse at work. Not only did I have to suffer through the abuse, but I also felt guilty for not saying anything sooner. In fact, one of my biggest regrets was to allow my boss to escape any scrutiny, meaning he was free to do it to someone else. I'm better at standing up for myself now. I'm much less of a pushover, but I'm still terrible at feeling my emotions and not repressing them.

Habits Checklist: Do you tend to repress your emotions, or do you express them? Do you feel allowed to stand up for yourself or does it bring guilt or shame? Have you ever exploded because you had been repressing too much or for too long?

WRONG TRIBE

"Hell is other people."
– Jean-Paul Sartre

I remember clearly the day I knew I was not meant to finish my PhD in physics. I was having a coffee in the break room of my office's floor and feeling pretty morose about my situation. All I wanted was to forget about my work, my boss, everything for fifteen minutes, before I had to go back and spend more hours on a project I hated.

In the break room sat two of my fellow PhD students with whom I hadn't particularly socialised before. I sat down with them, ready to vent or just chat and get distracted. But I caught up on their conversation and realised they were talking about the one thing I didn't want to hear: work. They were chatting about a computer

---

[6] Chapman, Benjamin P. et al., "Emotion Suppression and Mortality Risk Over a 12-Year Follow-up", https://www.ncbi.nlm.nih.gov/pmc/articles/PMC3939772/ (accessed 27 Feb. 2020)

programme they were writing, and how excited they were at the idea of finishing it. I sat in a corner, taken aback. These people were not faking it; you can't fake passion like that. They really enjoyed talking about physics and —gasp— really liked their job.

I felt like an alien. I hated my job at this point—due to the abuse from my boss, sure, but I also didn't enjoy the nature of the job at all. I had absolutely no passion for it and couldn't wait to get home to work on my fanfiction. I felt so lonely in this instant. I realised that, even if these people were supposed to be my peers, they were not my "tribe". They didn't have the same goals as me, the same interests or aspirations, and looked down on everyone who didn't share their passion for physics. That's when I knew I had to quit. Not just my particular lab and boss, but quit altogether. Science, PhD, all of it. I was not where I was supposed to be, and if I kept on going I would just make myself more and more miserable. And none of these guys would understand what was my problem.

The people who surround you are crucial to maintaining your mental health. I've written in my previous book about toxic people and how they bring you down no matter how much you try to get your head out of the water. And it's true! Keeping toxic people around you is the equivalent of eating something that you know will make you sick, over and over again, even though you know it's bad for you. One toxic person can damage your self-esteem, or stress you so much that you can develop genuine health problems.

But even without toxic people, the wrong entourage is a killer for your efforts. If you only surround yourself with people who don't share your interests, who don't understand your thoughts or don't share your goals, you are shooting yourself in the foot. Mental health is a group effort, and if the group dynamic is dysfunctional or if you are with the wrong people, your mental health can suffer.

A sign that you are not with the right people is keeping a lot of secrets, perhaps even the "real you", from your entourage. Feeling lonely all the time, never being able to talk to someone or having an unequal talking time (they vent a lot but you can never vent yourself) are all signs that something is wrong.

Habits Checklist: Let's assess your "tribe": do you feel accepted and supported by your family/friends/colleagues? Do you feel like you can talk to them when you feel down, or share your hopes and successes? If not, why not?

Never Saying No

"Please all, and you will please none."
– Aesop

From very early on in life, we are taught to accommodate other people, to be polite and help others as much as we can. And, as a whole, it makes for a world that is globally functioning (to a certain level). But problems start when you don't allow yourself put limits to others, out of politeness, out of habit or simply because you don't want to disappoint.

I'm totally guilty of this. I will bend over backwards to help people even if it's inconvenient to me. I like to think that I'm a good person, but sometimes I don't know when to say no.

People like me have a hard time establishing limits and applying them, which means that more often than not, we are taken advantage of. And we know it perfectly, which as a result brews resentment and anger against the other person, and especially against ourselves.

Limits are hard. Growing up in a house where my limits were constantly flouted, I have no idea how to uphold them in a way that doesn't make me feel guilty. I always have the feeling that I'm somehow insulting a person if I say "no", even if I really don't want to say "yes".

This has led to years of being a pushover, of being "too nice", of bottling up, of feeling like I'm worth less than other people and of extreme anxiety. For people like me, "just say no" doesn't work, because you are fighting years and years of conditioning to say "yes".

Habits Checklist: What is your relationship with limits? Are you a people pleaser? Do you overcommit, even when you know you should rest? When was the last time you said no to a friend or a

partner? How did it make you feel?

CONSTANTLY CONNECTED

"Cell phones are so convenient that they're an inconvenience."
– Haruki Murakami

One of the first things I do when I wake up in the morning is check Twitter, Instagram and Facebook. I see messages and feel obligated to reply immediately because seeing them means they are on "read'. I can't take an afternoon off without getting notifications or emails. Everywhere I go, I feel like I need to check my phone, in case I'm missing out on an important message. Switching off the phone feels almost illegal.

It's my own fault, of course. After all, I've build my social media profiles, in particular Twitter, to the point where I get notifications very regularly (around one every half hour on Twitter, even when I don't interact for a few days). But it doesn't mean that it is beneficial for my mental health.

There are more and more studies that link the "always on" culture that we have adopted since the advent of social media, and mental health issues such as depression and anxiety. It has devastating effects, especially at work[7], where employees don't feel like they can be completely "off" anymore and check their work emails even at home. I did it too, and it meant that I brought the stress from work home with me.

But even without talking about work, our "always on" mentality means that we can never catch a break; we can never "disappear" for a few days. A couple of decades ago, going on holiday meant being unreachable from everyone and everything. These days, it just means being pressured to post pictures of our feet in front of the swimming

---

[7] Moss, Rachel, "'Always On Culture Causing A 'Stress Epidemic' Among Brits—Here's How to Switch Off", *The Huffington Post* (2017), https://www.huffingtonpost.co.uk/entry/always-on-culture-causing-a-stress-epidemic-among-brits-heres-how-to-switch-off_uk_5a09769de4b05673aa5a6691 (accessed 27 Feb. 2020)

pool. Worse, we are in constant competition to post more, say more, interact more. It's like having a second job from which you can never clock off.

Social media can be an addiction, but it's not always treated that way. It is a tool that can lead to a poor self-image, numbing pressing matters and enabling avoidance of dealing with real problems. Even if we are aware that it doesn't help us, we don't really have a choice. Especially as an artist, social media is crucial for our career. For independent authors like me, social media is a key medium of free advertising for books and events. Without it, I'm nobody. It's ironic, really.

Habits Checklist: When was the last time you switched off your phone? Not just to restart it because it was buggy. Not just put in silent mode. Switched. Off. For several hours. A day, even, without checking any social media. Do you find it difficult to be completely disconnected from the world? Do you feel stressed if you haven't checked your account for a couple of hours?

Using Distractions

"Only put off until tomorrow what you are willing to die having left undone"
– Pablo Picasso

Do you often use Netflix or a video game or a book to distract yourself from a big problem or stress? We all do it, and to be honest, if this wasn't a thing, us creators of entertainment would not have a job. But there's a difference between a momentary distraction and constant numbing of pain and responsibility.

Otherwise called procrastination, using distractions to avoid facing problems head-on is a very common behaviour. It's not that we are lazy or that we don't manage our time well; it is actually an avoiding behaviour that can hurt in the long term.

Procrastination is a coping strategy which helps avoid stress or failure, but at the same time, it prevents us from starting to get better. It is different from inaction because it gives us the illusion that we are doing something, while nothing productive is actually getting done.

One of my favourite ways of procrastinating is to be really active on Twitter. I post a new tweet, I reply to followers, I add more people or remove others. A part of my brain gets satisfied because I'm doing something—I'm not being totally lazy. And even if deep down I understand that all of this is not a substitute for real work, I leave it at that.

At the heart of procrastination lies a self-esteem issue. I don't feel good enough, serious enough, talented enough to accomplish a certain task, so I'll delay it as much as I can, hoping that future me will be better equipped to deal with it, and try to forget about it in the meantime. This often makes me feel guilty or ashamed because I haven't done what I set to do. In a society that values productivity above everything else, procrastination is the ultimate shame.

Habits Checklist: Do you procrastinate often? Do you use distraction to avoid thinking about what you should do? If procrastination is your first reflex when facing a hard task, ask yourself: why is that?

SELF-DEPRECATION

"There's no room for demons when you're self-possessed."
– Carrie Fisher

The brain is a really weird organ. It can be so brilliant, and yet so stupid. It can come up with so many fantastic ideas but also believe incredibly stupid ones.

Take self-deprecation, for example. Being the butt of our own joke from time to time isn't the worst thing in the world. However, repeated often enough, our brain is going to start to believe all the nasty things we say about ourselves. It's almost a self-fulfilling prophecy gone wrong.

But why do we self-deprecate in the first place? Sometimes, the intention is to make other people laugh. There's nothing wrong with that, and the most beloved comedians do it on a regular basis. However, a lot of the time, self-deprecation is a way to fish for compliments. It's a poor attempt at disguising low self-esteem.

I know that often it is seen as an act of politeness to not gloat in a compliment. In some cultures, self-deprecation is even elevated as a virtue (for example, here in England, it is seen as something completely normal).

Self-deprecation is not modesty. It's not being humble. It's seeking external validation because you can't find it in yourself. When I say, "Oh Céline, you are so dumb sometimes," what I really hope to hear is someone replying, "Of course not, you're not dumb." And if that doesn't come, it makes me feel worse, and again my brain ends up believing whatever I feed it with my unfortunate words.

Self-deprecation is sometimes difficult to spot. A good tip to apply is to observe how you respond to compliments. Do you accept compliments, or do you feel the need to add a joke against yourself? People with low self-esteem find it impossible to respond to a compliment with a simple "thank you".

Habits Checklist: What is your go-to reaction to compliments? Is your humour only self-deprecating? And do you feel bad when someone else teases you, as you are the only one allowed to put yourself down?

DRAMA

"I need drama in my life to keep making music."
– Eminem

Some people thrive on drama. There is always something happening, always something wrong or someone with whom they have a feud. Whether it is at work, with friends or online, there is always a possibility for an argument.

Arguing with people constantly can come from the need of being the centre of attention, from the need for validation, or from the need to distract yourself.

In fact, you don't need other people to create drama. I catch myself imagining arguments with people all the time! One prime example is imagining a conversation with a difficult customer that I might have to deal with. Perhaps the customer is rude, or they are super demanding. I make up the conversation, how it would go, how they would respond, how it would escalate and end up in a big argument. Pure drama, all happening in my head, without anything prompting it.

And then I feel like crap because of what "happened" in my head. That's the problem with such a habit: you get so good at it that you *feel* exactly as if the argument had happened in real life. For your brain and your limbic system, it's as if you had that conversation. It makes no difference that you actually were taking a shower and didn't open your mouth. Sometimes, I replay real-life conversations and change how I would respond to them. I have the perfect comeback now, in hindsight. Or I say the things I wish I could say in real life but can't.

Drama, whether real or made up, can become an addiction. It creates a flux of adrenaline and makes you feel important, vindicated or powerful. Often, drama can make you feel excited, at least at first, but it can become exhausting to be embroiled in yet another fight.

Habits Checklist: Do you have a habit of arguing with people? Or do you catch yourself fighting with people in your head? Do you react to problems by acting out? Do you feel like fighting is the only way you can be heard?

TAKING EVERYTHING SERIOUSLY

"That is the key to navigating this life—don't take it too seriously. That's when the party begins."
– RuPaul

I used to see myself as a very serious person. I've studied physics, for goodness sake. I'm studious, I don't dawdle, I know what I'm talking about. I took myself deadly seriously, because seeing myself otherwise would invite jokes.

Taking yourself too seriously comes from a very real, deep fear of being ridiculed. We all, deep down, fear people mocking us. It's even more ingrained if you have been through experiences where people ridiculed you on a regular basis (for example, bullying). We never want to go through that again, so we guard ourselves so closely that we never let anything come in.

This fear is so strong that it can turn into a proper phobia: gelotophobia. It's the fear of being laughed at, and it's a type of social phobia. But without even reaching the level of phobia, this fear is responsible of depriving us of very important experiences. It can lead us to be withdrawn, appear cold, makes it difficult to form bonds with other people and can degenerate in violence.

Taking yourself too seriously can also paralyse your creative bones, make you incapable of innovating, of trying new things or publicising new ideas. As an artist, it can prevent you from trying "silly" things, venturing onto a different path and doing what you really want to do.

I still take myself too seriously from time to time, and I still avoid looking silly when I feel unconfident in myself. It's an everyday battle to see the humour in life and in my work. But I can immediately tell when I take a project too seriously: suddenly I don't dare to try new avenues, I feel withdrawn and I hate that my results are not perfect already.

Habits Checklist: What is your relationship with humour? Do you find that life is something to be taken seriously? Do you hate people who laugh at everything?

GIVING UP

"Our greatest weakness lies in giving up. The most certain way to succeed is always to try just one more time."
– Thomas Edison

I asked on Twitter if my followers had a particular habit that made their mental health worse. One of them gave a reply that really intrigued me: "slashing the other three tires". Meaning that giving up on your goal because of one setback is like slashing your other three tires because you got a flat.

In other words, if I already broke my diet and ate a cookie, I might as well eat the whole box and give up completely. It was not worth it to starting the diet in the first place, and I should stop. I am completely guilty of this. I set myself great goals, but at the first obstacle, I completely fold and give up, and it makes me feel absolutely terrible about myself. It's like the slightest setback can crumble all my efforts. One bad day can mean that the whole project is compromised, as it is seen as tainted.

Giving up too quickly is a symptom of a negative self-belief. It's as if you didn't believe you could do something from the beginning and use the first setback as an excuse to stop working on it. Worse, every setback following the first one will be seen as a confirmation of this belief.

Since every project will have its setbacks, this habit makes sure that you don't finish anything worthwhile, and reinforces your original belief that you can't do it. It's a vicious circle that gets worse over the years.

Habits Checklist: Are you guilty of "slashing the other tree tires" too? Do you give up as soon as an obstacle appears? Do you use any setback as an excuse?

CYNICISM

"What is a cynic? A man who knows the price of everything, and the value of nothing."
– Oscar Wilde

It's very easy to become cynical as an adult. I feel it too. The news is constantly negative, rich people get richer, poor people get poorer, and politics doesn't change a single thing; the climate will kill us all, and love is nothing but a chemical reaction.

Being cynical means that you fundamentally distrust the intentions of people around you. Everything that happens to you is seen through a distorted filter that makes you wonder, "What's the catch?"

It is often seen as the opposite of being naive, which seems like a good thing. Nobody in this day and age wants to be seen as naive or gullible. Being cynical is presented as a strength, as something you should be as you get older, almost as "cool".

But really, cynicism is not the opposite of being naive. It's the opposite of being hopeful—of being vulnerable. Of giving another chance, even when history or the news or your mother have proved you wrong time and time again.

Cynicism is a defence mechanism. It's our way of saying "I told you so" to the world when something bad happens. It's easier to be cynical than vulnerable, disappointed or angry. It's also a good excuse to do nothing to improve our situation because making changes won't work.

Of course, very often, cynics are right. Your neighbour didn't bake a pie for you just out of the goodness of their heart—they also wanted you to look after their cat for two weeks while they are away on holiday. But expecting every single interaction with others to be somehow negatively motivated makes your brain constantly see the worst aspects of a situation.

Cynicism trains your brain for depression. Research[8] suggests a strong link between a cynical hostility and depressive mood. Allowing yourself to dig deep into cynicism, even imposing it angrily on others, may lead to a situation where your brain can't find any positivity or hope. It is a slippery slope that we all have to deal with, as we are probably all cynics to a certain degree.

Habits Checklist: When something positive happens, do you immediately find the flaw? Do you think there's always a reason behind niceness? Do you believe that there's a "catch" behind good news?

---

[8] Nabi, H. at al., "Hostility and depressive mood: Results from the Whitehall II prospective cohort study", *Psychological Medicine*, vol. 40(3) (2010), pp. 405-413. Available online here: https://www.cambridge.org/core/journals/psychological-medicine/article/hostility-and-depressive-mood-results-from-the-whitehall-ii-prospective-cohort-study/76803E41FB196CED104304391C16FEEE# (accessed 27 Feb. 2020)

CHAPTER THREE

HOPES AND EXPECTATIONS

The Root of Change

After the previous chapter's overdose of junk habits, I could tell you that you just need to abandon these bad habits and adopt new ones. But that wouldn't be very useful because:

1. You probably already know that.
2. Breaking an old habit or building a new one is not as easy as it sounds.
3. You need a compelling reason to do it.

In this chapter, we are going to talk about reasons to change. You need a fighting chance in the battle against mental health issues. You need a drive, a motor, something that will still carry you to make positive changes that will last past the next few days.

We are also going to talk about your goals and aspirations, as well as debunking some crazy expectations that you might have.

Once this is done, you'll be ready for your new diet.

Why the Bad Diet?

If you have been to one of my workshops or read my blog, you know that I'm obsessed with one word: WHY?

To create real change, to achieve difficult goals, you need to understand what makes you tick. Your drive. The underlying reason why you do what you do. And in terms of mental health, you need to understand what the bad habits do to you before you can break them.

We don't do things repeatedly for no reason. If we adopt a behaviour or a set of actions that we know are bad, there is often an explanation. We are not stupid or deluded. I actually believe that most people are perfectly aware of what they are doing, but choose to do it anyway.

Let's go back to our junk food metaphor. Logically, I know that eating at McDonalds is bad for my health. I know it will only fill me up for a little while, and that I'll be hungry again in a couple of hours. I'm also aware that on the long term, it will clog my arteries and mess with my sugar levels. It's a fact, and I know it. But I do it because I am hungry, because I crave that pesky sugar rush and because it will give me satisfaction quickly and plainly. I don't have to cook, I don't have to pay too much and I get something filling and comforting. My reason to eat at McDonalds is, at the moment when I decide to buy, more compelling than the reasons to avoid it.

Now, let's examine the same situation, but in the context that I've just been told that my cholesterol level is likely to kill me within six months. Suddenly, the reason to avoid junk food is much more compelling than a brief moment of satisfaction and happiness. The facts about eating there haven't changed, but the scale has been tipped towards healthy eating because my circumstances have changed.

If you are using the workbook, open it to the third chapter. You'll see a table with all the bad habits that we have discussed previously. You can tick each habit that you have (or if you work on the computer, delete the habits that you don't have). For each habit, take a few minutes to write down the reasons why you do it. You don't need to be super detailed—just a sentence or two is enough.

For example: "I use self-deprecation so I can fish for compliments from other people". Be honest with yourself, because everything that comes after this will depend on the work you do here.

But what if you don't know why you do something? For example, I'm not 100% sure why I still hold a grudge against my former bosses. Then you can write guesses, such as, "I think it keeps me motivated in a weird way, but it could also be because I need a reason to explain why I feel depressed".

WHERE YOU WANT TO BE

Another very important concept that we need to talk about before making any change is: what are your goals? Where do you want to be?

It's funny because very few people have a crystal clear vision to answer to this question. Some people will have a ready answer, such as, "I want to become a published author", but most won't have a clear idea. Worse, for many people, it's too painful to set goals because you can't see yourself ever achieving them. This is especially true when it comes to mental health. I want to be happy, successful, less anxious and more confident, but I have no idea how that would look, and I have no faith that I will ever achieve it.

The problem with not having a clear image of where you are going is that you risk free-falling, going in the wrong direction or simply lacking motivation and direction.

I've noticed that every time I have felt like I had no goal, purpose, or objective to aspire to, my mental health took a turn for the worst. Goals and a healthy mental health are tightly linked, and it is important to take some time to think about what you want.

In your workbook, make a list of your goals related to mental health. Where do you want to be? What are you aiming for? For example my own goals are:

- Manage my anxiety so I can be productive most days
- Become better at loving myself and visualising a positive me
- Reduce the number of days where I'm too depressed to do anything
- Be confident enough to try new things on a regular basis

These goals are realistic because I think they are physically possible to achieve. Even if, for now, I don't necessarily believe that I'll ever get there. I could have written:

- Remove my anxiety

- Meditate like a pro for hours every day
- Never be depressed
- Try new things every day

But these goals are not realistic. Anxiety is not an illness that you can make disappear, and I know I can't sustain a heavy rhythm of meditation, new things and productivity without breaking down.

So, what are your goals? Are they realistic?

WHERE YOU SHOULD BE

We all have expectations about our lives. They are often developed as children, reinforced by the media and what society shows us. Then, often, they are revised or downgraded once we grow up.

As a teenager, I saw myself as a great and popular novelist, rich and famous. Then I had to revise my expectations when I had to find a job and earned very little money for a lot of annoyance. It seems to me that every few years, I have to downgrade my dreams, my expectations, and it hurts. Oh man, it hurts.

I will never be the youngest or most famous science fiction writer of a generation. I will never be the genius scientist who also wrote genius stories. I will also not be a millionaire any time soon, no matter how much I dream of it. With all these dreams and hopes, I expected to get to them eventually, and I didn't. Cue feelings of failure, of being a loser, of having completely destroyed my life.

Where you "should" be, what you "should" do, and who you "should" be is a natural way of thinking, but it's also extremely destructive when you compare your actual life to the dream you had imagined.

This section might seem completely contradictory to the previous one. After all, I've pushed you to establish goals because, without goals, your mental health is likely to deteriorate. And now, I'm telling you that these same goals can make you feel worse? Doesn't that seem contrary?

It actually isn't. The difference is that goals and expectations are not synonymous. Goals are objectives you are working towards. Expectations are what you think should happen to you. The first depends on you; the second depends on someone/something else. There is a big difference.

***LIFE IS NOT YOUR FAULT**

As a rule, you should not let your mental health depend on factors beyond your control. Of course, other people influence us, but leaving your happiness in someone else's hands is not a good recipe for success.

Following this, I think it's a good idea to observe and dissect what has made us who we are, and where we are right now. It is a mix of things we have done, and things that have happened to us, plus how we reacted to all of that. It's inevitable that, somewhere along the way, things didn't go as expected.

Make a list of the expectations you had when you were younger about where you should be today. Try to remember what you dreamed about, such as, "by the time I'm twenty/thirty/fifty, I'll be this". Did you achieve all of it? What happened along the way? What went right, and what went wrong?

Now make a list of all the things you have done that would have been completely unexpected for teenager-you. What have you done that you would have never thought about in a million years? Did you choose to go in a different direction than your early goals? Why? And what did it bring you?

This exercise is an important step when it comes to forgiving yourself, your past and who you are now, to start on a positive base. There might be choices that you made and that you deeply regret right now. I really regret studying physics, and even more so, attempting a PhD in that field. But at the time, I didn't know better. I didn't have enough information, maturity or help to make a different choice. That's okay, because my goals are still there, and while I had to give up on some of them, a lot of them are still achievable.

MEANING AND PURPOSE

I watched a TEDx Talk with Mark Leruste[9] recently that talked about the journey of an entrepreneur. I love reading and watching stuff about

---

[9] Leruste, Mark, *What they don't tell you about entrepreneurship*, https://www.youtube.com/watch?v=f6nxcfbDfZo (accessed 4 March 2020)

entrepreneurs because a lot of the advice that they give is also applicable to the life of an artist. And much like a lot of artists, entrepreneurs face a very difficult journey to success.

The talk had an interesting point of view about the struggles of entrepreneurship, such as loneliness and lack of direction. It all boiled down to one concept: purpose.

I think a lot of us struggle with mental health because we don't see a clear purpose to what we do. From purpose comes meaning, so without purpose, it's like our lives don't have meaning.

I have felt like that so often. Even though I love writing, and I felt compelled to do it, I didn't think it achieved a higher purpose than simply entertaining me and a few readers. Then I started The Part-Time Artist, and through that I found a real purpose to my work. Through my book, my podcast and my business, I help people. I've had so much feedback from people telling me that I've inspired them and that I've made them feel less lonely with their problems. It has become my purpose to reach more people and pass on my message.

This purpose gives a meaning to the many hours I spend writing, preparing a workshop or coaching someone. I feel like I make a difference.

If your life feels meaningless, you are at much higher risk of developing a mental illness[10]. If you feel like your life doesn't matter, that you make no impact, this is the first thing you need to sort out in order to feel happier and less burdened.

But it's very difficult to find a purpose or meaning, especially when the ugly head of depression or anxiety rears up. And it's even more difficult to keep up with it when things get tough. So let's address both.

---

[10] Glaw, X. et al., *Meaning in Life and Meaning of Life in Mental Health Care: An Integrative Literature Review*, https://www.ncbi.nlm.nih.gov/pubmed/27729687 (accessed 4 March 2020)

FINDING A PURPOSE

From the same TEDx talk that I discussed in the previous section, I got a very important insight about purpose and meaning. Most people make the mistake to try to answer the wrong question: "What is the meaning of life?" As if you should be able to answer a question that has agitated philosophers of the past few centuries in one afternoon.

Instead, you should ask yourself: "What is the meaning of *my* life?" The question might still feel nebulous, but at least it's a first step. To make it clearer to you, I'm going to list questions that will help you centre on finding the answer:

- What do I do all the time without feeling tired?
- What would I do if I had millions in the bank and didn't need to work?
- What do I do very well?
- What did I do last time I helped someone?
- What do I feel concerned about?
- What bothers me?
- What are my strengths?
- What makes me feel good about myself?
- What comes easily to me?
- What do people say about me that makes me feel accomplished?

You purpose might not be a simple, neat answer. Life rarely is that clean. Usually, our purpose is plural. I want to be able to help artists create more and be happier, and I want to entertain at the same time. I also want to influence young people about issues that I care about, while communicating my values to the people around me.

It's not an easy, quotable answer—and that's okay! The meaning of my life is not something I can tweet or make a gif about. I think most of us would like a simpler answer because it's easier to remember when things get tough. But for a lot of people, it doesn't go that way.

Purpose and meaning also change as you age. I was not much concerned about other artists years ago, until I became very active on social media and witnessed the suffering and anguish of so many people. The purpose that I have now would have been completely foreign to me years ago.

And purpose does not necessarily imply that you need to help people —or you might not see how it helps people in the beginning. That's also okay. It doesn't mean that you are a selfish person, just that it will probably be more difficult to see the results at first.

I think purpose is sometimes complicated by the fact that we are artists. We often confuse the purpose of a single piece with the bigger picture, the plan, the lifelong obsession. Make sure your purpose is not attached to a single project.

Take some time to answer the previous questions, and then try to summarise your answers in one or two paragraphs: what is the purpose of your life?

KEEPING UP WITH YOUR PURPOSE

Now that you have an idea of the meaning of your life, of your art and of what you do, let's talk about the second important part of this work: keeping track of it.

It is so easy to lose track of what meant so much to you. It's easy to think that your purpose, which previously felt so important, suddenly is less important because other more pressing events happen in your life. I've done this many times over.

The trick is to remind yourself, over and over, why you do what you do. Use visual or audio reminders of your purpose, of what it means to you.

For example, I keep every message from people who have said that my book, *The Part-Time Artist*, has helped them. When I feel down, when I feel like I am not accomplishing anything, I re-read them. They are the proof that I've had an impact on someone's life, that I'm not working for nothing.

I have also a fantastic boyfriend who forces me to remember the words of my readers when I feel down. He asks me, "What did that person say the other day?" and I begrudgingly repeat good feedback from a reader. It annoys me, because when I feel depressed or anxious, I don't want to remember the good things about my life, which is why he is so effective: he never lets me off the hook!

So, how are you going to keep your purpose fresh and alive? Do you prefer visual reminders, such as a frame on your desk with a few sentences reminding you why you are doing your art? Or perhaps you find it more efficient to repeat a mantra every day, which reminds you of your purpose? Take some time to design a way to keep your purpose alive, and make sure you include a contingency for when your purpose may change. For example, you can re-examine what you wrote about your purpose every year to make sure you are still connected to the meaning you give to your life, or to change some aspects of it.

GUILT

Hopefully, with this chapter, you understand a bit better what makes you "tick", what matters to you. Before we go into methods and strategy, I want to address one last concept that might completely ruin your new mental health diet before you even start: guilt.

Having mental health issues is still seen as extremely shameful, and doing something about it can be seen as selfish. In these conditions, it becomes very difficult to apply any practical advice about mental health.

While the stigma about mental health is not as bad as it used to be, it is still there. It may still feel shameful to go to a therapist or take a mental health day off work. We are still seen as "weak", we are still told that we should "tough it up". I bet you felt a bit ashamed buying this guide?

I want to make things very clear: to apply the principles in this book, to invest time and energy into your mental health, you are going to have to get over the guilt and shame that you might feel. You will have to battle the feeling of being selfish because you take time for yourself instead of someone else. You will have to stop feeling guilty because you said no to invitations. And it is very likely that someone along the way will try to put that shame back on you.

I want you to prepare yourself, especially if you are using this book purely as prevention. There will be people questioning why you are learning mindfulness techniques if you don't suffer from anxiety. There will be people who will shame you about your new routine, your new habits, perhaps even about seeking professional help.

It's up to you to be ready to counter them and banish guilt out of your life. Are you ready?

CHAPTER FOUR
YOUR NEW MENTAL HEALTH DIET

BUILDING NEW HABITS

In *The Part-Time Artist*, I wrote in detail about creating new habits and breaking old ones. In a nutshell, a habit is composed of three parts: the trigger, the routine and the reward. If you want to build a new habit, you need to think of a trigger and a reward that accompany your new routine, or you won't sustain it. Equally, if you want to break an old habit, you need to keep the old trigger but replace the old routine with a new one, keeping the old reward or finding a new one.

This is a very simplified but effective way of introducing a new routine in your life, such as writing, drawing or creating every day, and break old useless habits such as procrastination.

When it comes to habits linked to our mental health, however, a stronger approach is often needed. In particular, an extra step is added to the habit loop: thought reprogramming.

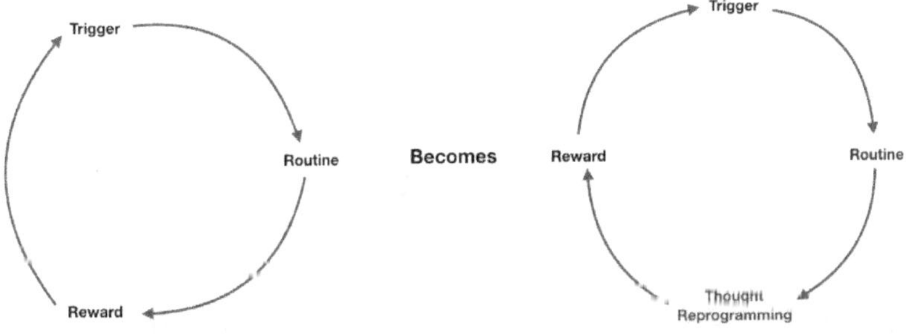

I will talk about thought reprogramming in the next section, but before that, another caveat: as opposed to a habit, such as smoking or eating junk food, you probably won't be able to rid yourself completely of a lot of mental health-related habits. For example, you will probably never get rid of your cynicism completely, or your ruminations. The best you can do is severely limit the time spent on these thoughts and make sure that the balance between supportive thoughts and destructive ones goes in your favour.

My best advice for this work is to tackle your habits one at the time. Don't try to get rid of all your bad habits and replace them with all the new habits right away. Identify the one bad habit that makes you suffer the most and try to limit it. For example, one of the worst habits for my mental health is to subject myself to negative news as soon as I get up. I therefore limit the time I spend on social media and news websites, and replace mainstream media with positive news websites. This is *one* change that can be made. You can work on something similar for a couple of weeks before changing something else.

Slow and steady wins the race. What we are trying to do here is create a lifelong change in your habits, so it's perfectly fine if you take a few months to apply all the changes.

The contents of this chapter are only suggestions. In the same way you probably don't have all the bad habits, you don't need to adopt all the good ones. Pick and choose what intrigues you, what you feel you can do, what you think will have the most impact.

THOUGHT REPROGRAMMING

You might have heard of Cognitive Behaviour Therapy (CBT) before, but perhaps you don't really know what it means. CBT is part of a family of psychotherapies called "Cognitive Restructuring" (CR) which aim to identify and correct thought patterns that are not productive.

The idea is to treat your brain very much like a computer: you have "shortcuts" to folders that you use a lot, so you can access them very easily. For now, they might all direct to the "bad thoughts" folders, because those are the ones you use the most. What CBT tries to do is to question why you have these shortcuts in the first place, remove the shortcuts and establish new shortcuts to "good thoughts" folders instead. And the more you use them, the more automatic it will be for you.

If you don't like the computer analogy, you can think about your brain like a big field that is crisscrossed with paths made by people who keep walking through it. Some paths are flattened and large, easy to use because they've been walked on a lot, while others are almost invisible in places because they are much less used. You want the paths to the productive thoughts to be large and clear, while the ones to the negative thoughts to be small and difficult to use. To do that, you'll have to walk the positive ones over and over and over, until they are large and nice and easy.

There are several ways of reprogramming your thoughts. Some can be done with a therapist and some can be done alone. There are books that detail the principles, as well as apps that can help you in the process.

The idea is roughly as follows:

<u>Step One</u>: Identify the thoughts that are not productive. This is the most difficult step. If you have never done this type of work, it can be very difficult to identify when your thoughts start to wander towards the negative or unproductive zone. But it is absolutely crucial. You need to be able to stop yourself and think "Oh, I'm thinking this unproductive thought again."

Try to train yourself to recognise the signs first, as it might be easier than constantly monitoring what you think. Do you feel suddenly in a bad mood, or significantly less motivated? What were you thinking just before that happened?

This work in itself can take several days or even weeks before you get the hang of it, depending on how aware you are of what you are thinking. You need to be able to recognise a thought that leads you down the rabbit hole of negativity as it occurs, or you won't be able to apply the next steps.

<u>Step Two</u>: Once you are aware of your unproductive thoughts, challenge them. You need to fact-check every one of these thoughts instead of taking them for granted. Ask yourself, "Is this true?"

This is where you need to be a bit tough with yourself and understand that what your brain produces is not necessarily true. You'll have to be a nitpicker. You need to poke holes in your brain's reasoning. For example, does your brain say, "you can never make friends"? Prove it wrong by thinking about the people you have befriended before. Or if your brain tells you that a particular person is so much better than you, challenge it by thinking about the times when you have been better than other people, or by saying that nobody is perfect.

At this stage, I need to warn you that your brain is not used to being contradicted. Whatever thoughts you are trying to rebut, they are going to defend themselves. For example, if you identify a voice that keeps coming back to sabotage you (your inner saboteur), it will be difficult to shut it up using only rational arguments. You are clever, which means that your inner saboteur is equally as smart. Most of the time, it will respond to your examples with rationalisations. It will say "but that's an exception" or "things have changed, you're not like that anymore". Logic itself might not be enough.

That's when separating yourself from your saboteur comes handy. Tell it to shut up. Out loud. I'm not joking. Your mission at this stage is to stop the unproductive thoughts one way or another, which means that you should use any tool available to you. Voicing your disapproval can be very powerful.

I call my inner saboteur Ralph. Giving a name to your saboteur allows you to take a distance from it and remove some of its power. You can also engage in a dialogue with it on a more "conscious" level, instead of letting the thoughts circle inside your head. If you are plagued with a saboteur that is relentless, naming it might help you. Separate yourself from it and see it for what it is: an annoying idiot who should not be allowed.

<u>Step Three</u>: Choose the thoughts you allow to thrive. You can make the decision to entertain constructive thoughts instead of destructive ones. You'll notice that I use the word "constructive" instead of "positive".

Complete and total positivity is usually impossible. You can't be positive no matter what happens, especially if it's not your natural personality. Your mind will reject it. When I say "constructive" thoughts, I mean "thoughts that will help you move forward".

For example, let's say that you are preparing to release a book and you feel anxious:

- Destructive thought: "Nobody will read it" – it's final, it's gloomy and there's nothing to do to change that
- Positive thought: "It's going to be super successful" – it's too generic, there's no proof or strategy, your brain will probably not believe it
- Constructive thought: "It's time to learn marketing to ensure this book is a success" – it's open, it's a strategy and it's believable

This is a mental exercise that is very difficult at the beginning because it feels fake. Your brain will probably remind you every step of the way that you are deluding yourself. But if you do it systematically, you'll notice a shift in your thought patterns. You'll "enlarge" the paths in your brain-field to constructive thoughts. You'll use the positive shortcuts instead of the negative ones.

REFRAMING

We have talked in the previous section about how you can challenge your negative thoughts and only pick up the productive ones. Now we are going to attack thoughts that limit your experiences, how you feel and how you are. These are known as limiting beliefs.

Limiting beliefs are things that you believe about yourself, about a situation or other people. They affect how you see the world and interpret the things that happen to you. Let's take an example: for years, I believed that it was impossible to earn money from writing. This particular belief came from my upbringing, and it shaped my life. It is the reason why I had a string of jobs I hated, why I studied science rather than creative writing, why I only made a try at it in my thirties. So many years were wasted not doing what I really yearned to do, because I believed it was impossible.

Limiting beliefs are not exactly thoughts. You don't actively think them —they are just there. They are as real as practical beliefs such as "I should never cross the road without looking left and right" or "I can't fly". These beliefs protect you and give you a safe framework to live in. The difference is that limiting beliefs actively prevent you from doing something without a real factual base, an explanation for why it is impossible.

Have you heard of the story of the four-minute mile? For years, centuries even, people thought it was impossible to run a mile in less than four minutes. The record was four minutes and a second, and stayed so for years. It was said that going under four minutes was just not possible for the human body, that it was the limit. In 1954, Roger Bannister broke the four-minute barrier and ran the mile in 3:59. And then, what happened? Suddenly, a bunch of people were able to break that barrier too. Roger Bannister destroyed the limiting belief that the human body couldn't run that fast.

> *"It always seems impossible until it's done."*
> *– Nelson Mandela*

In other words, how life works and how you think life works are two different things. Have you had the situation, as a child, when you went to a friend's house and wondered why some rules were different? For example your parents forbade you to do some things that were allowed by your friend's parents. It might have been a shock for some of you, but it might also have been liberating to see that some things are not necessarily true or impossible. Now, you need to do the same work with the limiting beliefs that you have.

First, identify the beliefs that prevent you from being happy, from evolving, from exploring new aspects of your art or are simply holding you back. This identification process will be the hardest step, as very often, we are not aware that these beliefs are limiting us.

Try to think about your dreams and the barriers that your mind puts between you and them. Examine also your behaviour in different aspects of your life—relationships, finances, art-making, health, fun—

and try to see if some core beliefs might influence how you behave in a negative way. Think how different your behaviour would be if you didn't have that particular belief. Would your life be better? Then it's probably a limiting belief.

Look for blanket statements, such as "I'll never be successful", or "people like us don't have a lot of money", or "what I create is never good enough". Look for other people's voices in your head, such as your parents or guardians telling you that something is impossible or that's "how things are".

This identification process is going to take time. I heard of reframing five years ago, and I still identify toxic beliefs that I have to this day. You will not be able to reframe everything at the same time, so start with one limiting belief, the most obvious one. The more you identify beliefs that don't serve you, the better you'll get at it.

The second step is to question the validity of these beliefs that you have identified. Similar to thought reprogramming, you'll have to fact-check and present evidence of the opposite. You are a lawyer representing yourself, and it's your job to search for counter-examples to prove your beliefs wrong. For example, when I thought that I could never earn money from my writing, I researched authors who make money from their books. I studied them; I researched what they did and how they succeeded. I presented my brain with so much evidence that it was indeed possible to earn a living from writing that my brain had to relent. That belief was wrong.

The final step is to build new and productive beliefs. For that, you need to research proofs that your new beliefs are more true than the old ones. You can compare a new belief to a table: it needs to have legs to stand tall and proud, and support the thoughts that you will lay on top of it. To make tall and steady legs, you need to prove to yourself that this new belief is true, over and over. In my case, the legs of my new belief were all these successful authors that I had studied, how they established their author business and how they functioned. When I start doubting that I can succeed, I go back to these "legs" and remind myself why I believe success is possible.

Reframing your beliefs will help you select supportive thoughts and generate better ones. It will also help you get rid of some of the toxic inner voices that you might have picked up along the way, as a child or an adult.

FORCED POSITIVITY

I know I've written that "positive" thoughts will not necessarily help you reprogram your thoughts. Positivity, however, can help you filter the information that you receive. In other words, if you search for positive stuff, you'll find that there is more of them than you think.

Mainstream media is skewed in a way that shows us only the worst and most sensational aspects of what is happening in the world. Good deeds and positive news are not "newsworthy" for most editors, unless they can twist it into a negative. In that context, you have to actively search for good news and uplifting events because they won't come to you automatically.

You need to "un-skew" the results, tip the balance back towards positivity, or your brain will end up believing that there's only negativity and crime and horror in this world. Every day, you need to remind yourself that the world is not just all dark and death. There is positivity.

"Frodo: What are we holding on to, Sam?
Sam: That there's some good in this world, Mr. Frodo. And it's worth fighting for."

– The Lord of the Rings: The Two Towers

It is your job to search for light even when everything seems gloomy. It is your job to notice good deeds and happy moments, if only to show your brain other stuff than the everyday doom and gloom of the news.

In the spirit of balance, one of the best services that you can do to your brain is to feed it less toxic doom-and-gloom sensational news, and give it some nuggets of positivity. Some websites, such as the Good News Network[11] and Upworthy[12] can help you with that.

My favourite thing to do is to read about progress in science. It gives me hope that we are progressing, that diseases like cancer or AIDS might one day be eradicated. It shows me people who don't live in the constant "everything is doomed anyway" mindset, and who do something to make the world better. I also like to follow positive

---

[11] The Good News Network: https://www.goodnewsnetwork.org/
[12] Upworthy: https://www.upworthy.com/

people on social media, who show me that success and happiness can be achieved, and inspire me to think better.

This work is not something you can just do once and be done with it. It's a conscious, repeated effort, the same way you eat healthy food repeatedly to feel better or become healthier. Your cynical self will probably rebel at the beginning, and say that the good never balances the bad of this world. To which I would reply, "It's still worth fighting for."

Morning Briefing

What do you do first thing in the morning? Do you snooze your alarm clock several times, then wake up late, rush through getting ready, barely eat anything, and leave for work in a bad mood? That's me, pretty much every day. These kinds of mornings prepare my mind for a terrible day, full of frustrations, longing for my bed, annoyed at everything and everyone.

Believe it or not, there's another way to start your day. Famous coach Tony Robbins calls it "priming", but I call it "morning briefing", because it reminds me of how I used to brief my team in the theatre before every show, making sure everyone was ready and in good spirits.

The content of the briefing will depend on how much time you have, on your preferences and on your lifestyle. If you're a parent who has to get three kids ready for school, perhaps you won't have time to spend an hour doing this.

But in general, briefing should have three components:

1. Physical
2. Grounding
3. Coaching

The first component, physical, is to keep you attuned to your own body. If you do this just after waking up, it gives you a good boost for the day to come. For example, you could do some light exercise for twenty minutes, or stretch for five minutes. The idea is to get you moving, to counter the inactivity and sluggishness that otherwise risks following you for the rest of the day. The length of time depends on your capacities and time available. If you are not a very active person, I recommend taking it easy, at least at first.

The second component, grounding, is all about linking your brain to your body, here and now. It can be concentrating on your breathing for a few minutes, meditating, imagining the flows of energy going though you, or simply staying quiet and calm for a little while. Taking a moment to live in the "now" is a very important aspect of mindfulness (we will discuss this later), and a very good way to start your day.

I have found that grounding is a great way to change your mood if you have frequent nightmares. I often (several times a week) dream about things that upset me or put me in a bad mood, a mood that can continue throughout the day. I need a clean break between night and day, and grounding is the best way I've found to do it.

Finally, the third component of the briefing, coaching, is about projecting yourself into your day and making sure that you have all the information you need to succeed. It is also time to think about the things that you have to do that might stress you out and try some visualisation based around them going well. Coaching is also time when you can imagine further into the future, your future successes, your plans working and your dreams being achieved.

Projecting into the future after being grounded in the present is powerful, but only if you do it in a positive way. Again, the idea is not to be naive and imagine all sorts of unrealistic possibilities, but to give yourself a pep talk, the same way you would to others before they have an important exam or perform a challenging task. This is where you get to be your own coach, where you remind yourself how you've accomplished great things before and that you can do it again

The way you do these three steps is entirely up to you, and I highly encourage you to try different things. Some people might enjoy coaching themselves out loud in front of the mirror, or while they are having a shower. Some might feel too shy to do it out loud and do it in the form of a directed meditation instead.

There's no right or wrong here. You don't even have to do it as soon as you wake up, if like me you need coffee first to be entirely operational. The only principle to respect is to never have a day again when you haven't made at least a little effort to brief yourself so you don't feel completely unprepared and overwhelmed for the day ahead.

BREAKS

I am the *worst* when it comes to taking breaks. I constantly overwork myself, and I don't take a break for many reasons: guilt, stress, anxiety, poor time management or even pressure from other people.

But if you want to improve your mental health or mood, taking breaks is *the* quickest and most efficient way to do it. Whether these are short breaks that you take during the day, longer breaks once a week or even longer ones once a year, it is important to not neglect them. Otherwise, it's almost guaranteed that your body or your brain will force you to do it.

Have you ever felt completely burned out, and caught a nasty cold that forced you to stay in bed for a few days? That was your body screaming at you to rest. Have you ever felt so tired that you couldn't concentrate, to the point where you ended up making a big mistake? That was your brain sending you the same message.

Now, I know that telling you to take a break will not make you take one. I know it because I frequently have to fight against myself to take one. It's very difficult to go against everything that you are, everything that perhaps you have been taught, to "self-indulge" by resting. Society is even rigged against us in this matter: who hasn't been made to feel guilty by an employer because you took a break during the day? Or took a few sick days to rest after a cold?

To apply this part of the "diet", you will need to be very strict with yourself and other people. I believe that the best way to take break is to plan them and make them part of your routine, instead of improvising and feeling guilty.

For example, when I worked in my previous job, I tried to take always breaks at the same time of the day. That way, I taught myself, and also other people, that at this time I would be taking five minutes for myself and that I didn't want to be disturbed. It worked, even if I was in a place where the culture was terrible and employees were pressured to eat lunch in front of their computer while still working. Nowadays, I write in big bold letters "day off" on my weekly planner, under at least one day. I am not allowed to have a week without a day off, except in very exceptional circumstances. And every January, I also plan a "me" weekend. I go somewhere, completely by myself, to breathe, rest and think about my goals for the year.

Everyone needs breaks. No one is immune to overworking and exhaustion, and it's better to include breaks into your routine now, instead of waiting and having to recover from a burnout (which can take months!).

Now, what do you do during your breaks? Do you stare at your phone and just let the time pass? Or do you stress, thinking about the pile of work that is waiting for you when you come back? Do you spend your entire weekend doing nothing and feeling like you are wasting your time, or do you make a point to do a lot of stuff, sometimes at the risk of coming back to work on Monday more exhausted than you were when you left?

Planning your breaks should also include a part of planning how you will spend this time off. Short breaks at work? Why not walk to another room, another part of the building or, if it is possible, outside?

One or two days off a week? Always include a "resting" phase and a "fun" phase into them. Perhaps sleeping in a little bit later, then doing an activity that makes you happy. I am aware that typical weekends in a typical household also involve a bunch of chores and unpleasant things, but these don't have to be the *only* thing that you do. Bummed out about having to clean your flat? Make sure you do something that you enjoy afterwards. Can't sleep in because you have kids? Then for once go to bed when they do to ensure that you have a good night's rest.

These are only some ideas of how you could make your breaks better, but it's up to you to find what really works with your life, with how much time you can realistically get and with your personality. A few years ago, a good day off involved going out and partying the night before, then sleeping in for most of the next day. It worked for me at the time, and it made me happy. I don't do this anymore because I've changed and I don't really like clubbing as much. You are allowed to test, try new things and improve your breaks little by little.

As long as you remember the most important: you need some time off!

DAYDREAMING

I'm going to ask you a personal question: when was the last time you went to the bathroom for… hum… a number two, and didn't take your phone with you? When was the last time you did nothing on public transport: no book, no music, no games? And when was the last time you just sat and got lost in your thoughts, without actively doing anything else?

It's been a while? Me too.

Daydreaming, or "mind-wandering", is generally seen as negative, and in the field of mental health it is studied for its negative consequences. Indeed, if you suffer from Maladaptive Daydreaming[13], you might spend hours and hours dreaming away your life, inventing scenarios and feeling emotions related to these scenarios, instead of actually living.

I believe, however, that you need to be able to daydream a little every day to keep track of yourself, of your thoughts and creativity. It is incredible the ideas that you can come up with, if only you stop giving your brain so much stimulation all the time! As a creative person, you

---

[13] Soffer-Dudek, Nirit and Eli Somer, "Trapped in a Daydream: Daily Elevations in Maladaptive Daydreaming Are Associated With Daily Psychopathological Symptoms", Front Psychiatry, vol. 9 (2018), pp. 194. Available online: https://www.ncbi.nlm.nih.gov/pmc/articles/PMC5962718/ (accessed 5 March 2020)

need a certain degree of boredom to allow your mind to work in the background and create new ideas. This is why people say they have their best ideas in the shower!

In today's world, however, we don't give ourselves the chance to do nothing, even for a few minutes. Everything needs to be multitasked, or we get bored.

Dare to get bored once in a while. Stop watching a video every time you brush your teeth or eat breakfast. Look out of the window and let your imagination wander. A recent study[14] suggested that, in small doses, daydreaming for a few minutes is actually very helpful in raising your productivity and your attention at work.

But what do you do if your mind systematically goes to negative thoughts when you daydream? You might want to start with the thought reprogramming method to try to shift your thought patterns. Another tool that might help you is to have a finite time for daydreaming. For example, set an alarm, and only allow yourself five minutes of mind-wandering. A short period of time spent daydreaming will still give you the benefits with less chance of turning negative.

HEALTHY LIFESTYLE

We literally talked about the opposite in Chapter 2, and I'm pretty sure that you know that to feel better inside, you need to live a healthy life. But how does one do that exactly?

Of the habits to change that will benefit your mental health, this will probably be one of the hardest, because unhealthy lifestyle and mental health issues feed off each other and maintain a vicious circle of unhappiness and unhealthiness. I eat junk food because I feel depressed, and the junk food ends up depressing me more, and so on.

---

[14] Merlo, Kelsey et al., "A Qualitative Study of Daydreaming Episodes at Work", Journal of Business and Psychology (2019). Available online: https://www.researchgate.net/publication/330092035_A_Qualitative_Study_of_Daydreaming_Episodes_at_Work (accessed 5 March 2020)

It is, however, one of the most concrete steps that you can make. The high you get after running, cycling or lifting weights is difficult to reproduce otherwise. When you eat healthy food, there's also a great feeling of being proud of yourself for doing a good thing, which in turn helps you feel more in control of your life and happier.

The tricky part is to keep on going over time. Eating one healthy meal is easy. Doing it for a week or a month is much more difficult. Going to bed at a reasonable hour when you are exhausted, easy. Doing it consistently every day, much less tempting. And hitting the gym seems like a good idea in January, but becomes a pure chore by February.

My trick—and the only thing that has ever worked for me—is to start small. I can't suddenly start running every day for an hour, or throw away all junk food and only eat salad. Every time I've been able to make lasting changes to my life, I've done it by small increments. I've recently started exercising almost every day, or at least every other day, and I only got to that point because I began with exercising for ten minutes only. I left the habit some time to develop and stick before I changed anything else.

When it comes to being healthy, I firmly believe that we often try to do too much too fast. Our body and mind don't have time to adapt to the change. It's too much, so we revert back to what was familiar. Your mission is to create a new "familiar" feeling, and for that, you need to do it slowly, over a long period of time.

If you think that your lifestyle influences your mental health for the worse, try to change *one* thing and stick with it for three weeks minimum. Document how you feel, the improvements you note, and perhaps the thoughts that try to push you to revert back. Once you feel like this is the new normal, then try changing something else.

MIND EXERCISES

In this section, I'm going to talk about techniques and exercises that are dedicated to your mind. Whether it is meditation, visualisation, mindfulness or gratitude exercises, they all have a purpose in making you feel better and training your mind to stay in the state of "better" over time.

I've talked about gratitude and meditation in my previous book, as these are two exercises that I try to do regularly, even if I'm not good at either of them. And "being good at it" is really not the point. Many people try meditation and give up because they can't stop themselves from overthinking or fidgeting. The point is not to become a perfect meditation guru. The point is just doing it. That's it.

So here's a simple meditation exercise that my therapist taught me that helped me tremendously and that anyone can learn to do very easily:

1. Sit down, back straight on a chair, hands on your knees. Close your eyes.
2. In your mind, visualise every part of your body one after the other, and make a conscious effort to relax them. It's easier to start with your face and concentrate on unclenching your jaw and relax your brow. Then go to the neck, the shoulders, the arms, the hands, the torso, the belly, the legs, the feet. You will probably want to fidget while doing this—that's okay!
3. Once your body is completely relaxed, concentrate on your breathing. Inhale, exhale.
4. You might find that at this point your mind is starting to wander away. That's okay too! Gently bring your thoughts back to your breathing every time they run away.

You might have to do this last step quite a lot, in fact, but make sure you do it gently and nicely. Don't be mad at yourself every time you have to do this, because the real training is not to think about nothing. It's to learn how to stop your mind wandering and bring it back to a neutral thought. The more you do this exercise, the better you will be at it and it will help a lot when you practice thoughts reprogramming, positivity and daydreaming.

In terms of gratitude, this is a subject that is slowly being studied by scientists and psychologists, and the results are very encouraging. According to one study[15], including a gratitude habit into the life of psychotherapy patients not only improved their mental health, but the benefits also accrued over time. In other words, not only is gratitude good for you, but it will make your mental health better and better as you keep on doing it.

You might wonder, how can I be grateful if my life is very difficult at the moment? Gratitude is not easy, especially if you are going through a hard time. It is, however, possible to make it a habit like any other by starting small. The first few times I did this, I looked around me and found three objects that I used frequently and wrote that I was happy that they existed because they made my life easier. It's an easy step that felt less cringy to me when I started. You can also list three names of people that you are thankful to have met in your life. Or three recent events that happened to you that made you happy.

The content is much less important than the mechanism. The idea is to turn your thoughts to something different than complaining. It's easy to think that everything is out there to get you, I completely understand that. This is to counter all these anxious and negative thoughts.

The best way to build the habit is either to integrate it into your morning briefing, as an extra step, or you can have a gratitude journal

---

[15] Wong, Y. Joel et al., "Does gratitude writing improve the mental health of psychotherapy clients? Evidence from a randomized controlled trial", *Psychotherapy Research*, vol. 28(2) (2018). Available online: https://www.tandfonline.com/doi/full/ 10.1080/10503307.2016.1169332?needAccess=true (accessed 5 March 2020)

in which you write every day the things you are grateful for, perhaps before going to sleep. The important part here is to do it often enough.

Visualisation can work as an addition to a meditation, or on its own as a regular way of thinking. I particularly use visualisation when I feel like a failure and like I'm never going to be successful. One of the most important components of visualisation is not to imagine a potential successful future for you. It's to *feel* it. That's why I think the name "visualisation" is badly chosen. If you only visualise a great future, it's going to feel fake and artificial, impossible to achieve. Your "realistic" self will fight against it and present with you a plethora of reasons why it won't happen to you.

However, if you feel like you would feel when you achieve your dreams, it's a totally different ballgame. Your inner saboteur is powerless against feelings such as happiness, pride and a sense of connection. If you train yourself to feel these kinds of emotions on a regular basis and associate them with your future success, it will help you feel more hopeful and probably more motivated too.

It can be hard to practice visualisation without feeling silly. It's much easier to imagine one concrete scenario instead of staying vague. I personally use a lot the "future interview" method, in which I imagine myself being interviewed about the things that I achieved. Depending on what I'm concentrating on, it could be a podcast interview, an interview at a science fiction convention, or even a TV interview if I feel bold! But start small if you feel like you really can't believe something bigger. In the "interview", I reflect on how difficult it was to achieve that big project, but that I succeeded anyway. I see myself giving advice to people who want to do what I "achieved", which is really me giving advice to myself from a place of happiness and success, instead of having the old nagging saboteur giving me bad advice.

Finally, let's talk about mindfulness. Mindfulness is a technique that brings your attention to the present moment, without judgment or expectation. Technically, meditation is a way to bring mindfulness, but you don't necessarily need to meditate to bring mindfulness.

I personally have found that mindfulness is most effective when I feel overwhelmed, on the verge of a panic attack or extremely anxious. In these situations, I might be too anxious to start meditating right away, which is what tripped me initially when I tried to regularly meditate. Mindfulness can be a quick way of grounding you, or a good way to prepare yourself for a meditation session.

My therapist taught me this nifty trick that I used at work when my bosses were horrible to me. Look at your feet. I'm serious, look at them. See how they work, how they look, how they walk, what kind of shoes you are wearing (if any). Detail them. Nothing else is more important than your feet. Try to describe them in as much detail as you can. You can do something similar with pretty much anything. I like using crystals sometimes, looking at them, touching them, feeling how smooth or how rough they are against my skin. To be honest, this can be done with any type of object.

The idea is to force yourself to return to the present moment. When you feel depressed or anxious, your mind tends to fly either to the past or to the future, and it becomes impossible to control. When the focus is on the present, your mind is much easier to calm down and reason with. When your attention is in the present, your mind has far fewer weapons to hurt you.

There are loads of different methods[16] and mindfulness-based therapies[17], and if you are interested, you might want to research the subject and test these methods. What is important is that mindfulness-based techniques are proven[18] to be effective when it comes to helping with mental health issues.

---

[16] Swansea Bay University Living Life Well Programme: http://www.wales.nhs.uk/sitesplus/863/page/47545 (accessed 5 March 2020)

[17] NHS BeMindful Programme: https://www.nhs.uk/apps-library/be-mindful/ (accessed 5 March 2020)

[18] Coronado-Montoya, Stephanie et al., "Reporting of Positive Results in Randomized Controlled Trials of Mindfulness-Based Mental Health Interventions", https://journals.plos.org/plosone/article?id=10.1371/journal.pone.0153220 (accessed 5 March 2020)

GIVING BACK

When I asked on Twitter for tips on improving mental health, one person mentioned that helping other people made her feel better. Whether it is giving money to a charitable cause or helping a neighbour, it seems that cultivating generosity is a good way to alleviate symptoms of depression and anxiety.

This is a sector of psychology that is not much researched, but I found a study[19] that examined the brains of people who gave to charities and found that philanthropy activates regions of the brain that are associated with pleasure, trust and connection. When you help someone, you don't just imagine feeling good. Your brain literally fires the "feel good" zones. Other researchers talk about the "helper's high,"[20] as helping people apparently releases dopamine in your brain, which increases your happiness level. Some studies[21] show that, all in all, helping others might be even more effective than giving yourself treats.

Does that mean that you should give up all your free time and help everyone who needs it? No, because not only is that impractical (there are so many causes to help), but also it might have the opposite effect. Indeed, if you tend to feel like everyone is already taking advantage of you, it will make it worse.

So, how to find the right balance? First, research one or two causes that you really care about. This is where a lot of people get it wrong: you might tend to donate or help causes because they seem important or urgent, but they don't necessarily mean something for you. Again,

---

[19] Moll, Jorge et al., "Human fronto–mesolimbic networks guide decisions about charitable donation", *Proceedings of the National Academy of Sciences,* October 17, 2006 103 (42) 15623-15628. Available online: https://www.pnas.org/content/103/42/15623 (accessed 5 March 2020)

[20] The Helper's High: https://greatergood.berkeley.edu/article/item/the_helpers_high (accessed 5 March 2020)

[21] Nelson, S Katherine, Kristin Layous and Steven W Cole, "Do unto others or treat yourself? The effects of prosocial and self-focused behavior on psychological flourishing", *Emotion,* vol. 16(6) (2016). Available online: https://escholarship.org/content/qt7pf57270/qt7pf57270.pdf?t=oo8oy9 (accessed 5 March 2020)

there are many crisis in this world that you could help with, but you can't do everything! You have to choose, and it's always better to choose something that means a lot to you.

For example, I tend to donate to charities that help homeless people. The reason is that when I used to work in the West End in London, I would see dozens of homeless people sleeping rough around the theatres. After a while, I got familiar with them. I saw them every day on the way to work, said hello, and would worry when one of them was absent for too long. It would have been impossible for me to give each of them money every day, so I chose a homelessness charity that I knew was working in the area, to help them as much as I could.

Did it change the world? No. Not at all. But I hope it helped some of them, at least for a while. It made me feel like I was doing something towards a problem that I really cared about. Even when I felt anxious about everything else, at least that was something I could do properly and help.

If finances are tight, you don't necessarily need to give money. You can give your time, fundraise or publicise charities on social media. I notice very often that when my life feels uncontrollable, out of focus and meaningless, just doing something nice for someone, for no particular reason, helps me feel calmer and more hopeful.

SPIRITUALITY

I'm a scientist. I studied physics for years because I wanted to understand how things functioned. I refused to be a dumb person who believed dumb things, like the Bible or that God had done this or that. For years, I was as atheist as you can be. As a teenager, I refused to even go into churches and rolled my eyes at religious ceremonies of any kind.

A couple of years ago, though, I visited Rome, went into the Vatican, and even prayed in St Peter's Church. Currently, I'm an agnostic. I don't believe in any god, but I believe in the idea that there are things higher and more complex than me, and that the universe means something, even if our human level of intelligence hasn't reached a point of understanding it. So, what happened to change my mind so radically?

First, the young adult that I was went through two years of psychological abuse that seemingly served no other purpose than to destroy me. Then, the know-it-all scientist had to face that even her biggest role models in the field admitted to not knowing everything.

But what really made me explore my spirituality was the fact that it made me feel better. It's as simple as that. Reflecting on bigger concepts such as the meaning of life and humanity, and connecting with other spiritual people are just a few methods that I've found to keep my anxiety in check.

Faith is a subject that is very well studied[22]: spiritual people tend to have better connections with others, have more support, a more active social life and better mental health. When I was an atheist, I thought that people just enjoyed deluding themselves, but now I think it is a much more complex process that links our beliefs and our minds.

This section is not meant to convince you to convert to any religion. My point is that groups linked spiritually can be a fantastic supportive environment. So, if you are already a believer, try to take the time to examine your faith, to perhaps engage in social activities within your religion (church, mosque, temple, etc). If you are not spiritual, perhaps you can try to replace these connections with activities that bring you together with people with similar interests and values.

BETTER CONNECTIONS

Since we are talking about making connections with people, I think this is also an area that you can concentrate on to improve the way you feel.

Good relationships are vital for your mental health. Not only can they

---

[22] Koenig, Harold G, "Research on Religion, Spirituality, and Mental Health: A Review", *The Canadian Journal of Psychiatry* (2019). Available online: https://journals.sagepub.com/doi/abs/10.1177/070674370905400502 (accessed 5 March 2020)

give you a sense that you belong somewhere, they also form the support systems that will pick you up when you trip and help you whatever the circumstances. Unfortunately, we live in an age where having a close-knit community around us is rarer and rarer. We might struggle to find a partner, but often we also struggle simply finding friends.

Friendships are difficult. And sometimes the more you age, the least friends you seem to have. It's something I've noticed in my own life, and many people have realised the same thing. Not only do you lose sight of a lot of friends, because you get trapped in the cycle of work-commute-sleep, but you might get less opportunities to make significant connections with new people.

I have experience with both of these problems. When I moved for the first time out of my native Belgium, I made a point to return to my hometown every couple of months and invited all my friends to have a drink every time I came back. At first, it seemed everything was going well. Then the number of people who showed up dwindled until I only was able to gather one or two people at a time. It hurt me a lot. I felt like a terrible friend because I could not be there every day to see them, and at the same time, I resented them because they would not take the time to see me when I was back. Nowadays, after over ten years living abroad, I have kept contact with only a handful of people.

> *"People come into your life for a reason, a season, or a lifetime."*
> *– Anonymous*

I have a hard time making new friends too. Working mostly from home dramatically reduces the number of people that I meet and can socialise with. But even when I was working full-time, this was an issue. I didn't seem to be able to transform casual relationships into friendships. Like many people, I have a lot of Facebook friends, but not many people I can actually call when I feel down.

Seeing that this problem didn't solve itself, I decided to actively do something about it. First, I sought to understand why I have such a hard time making meaningful connections with people. If you are in the same situation, you might want to take some time to examine yourself and ask yourself the same question. Sometimes the answer can be easy, such as not seeing people often enough to establish a friendship. Sometimes it is deeper than that. I find it extremely difficult to trust people, and therefore I never share anything about myself, which in turn prevents them from really knowing me.

The way we build friendships is directly impacted by how we have learned to build relationships in the first place. I know that my defiance of anyone new directly comes from my childhood, and how I couldn't confide in anyone without being mocked for what I liked and who I really was. In my mind, giving information about myself to someone equals giving them weapons to hurt me in the future.

Whatever your answer is, you need to be aware of how you behave with people who could potentially become a friend, so you better understand their reactions to you.

Secondly, I realised that, as an adult, I need to put effort into my friendships, both new and existing. When I was at school, it was easy. I would see my friends every day and it didn't require any particular effort on my part. As an adult, this isn't true anymore, unless you are lucky enough to be friends with someone at work. More often than not, you need to make plans to see one of your friends—and that's where you need to put in some work. Days, weeks, sometimes months can pass before you realise that you haven't seen a certain person. It's up to you to actively make plans and stick to them. It's up to you to contact them and make sure you keep the connection alive.

But what if I'm the only one making an effort? This is a valid question, and I'm sure you have found yourself in situations where you were always the one keeping in contact, making plans, and that if you didn't do anything, you would never see this person. Well, I don't have a clear answer for you. Some people are worth making more effort for, and some people aren't. It is important to communicate what you need and how you feel to them, and see how they react. Sometimes, an honest conversation will resolve these types of situation.

Friendships are a delicate balance between putting in work and getting comfort in return. If one side of the scale is tipped, it doesn't work. It's the same if you are always the person demanding too much from your friends—if they are only there to help you, but you don't give anything in return.

This brings me to the third step: making better connections sometimes means dropping crappy ones. Some friends will make you constantly feel terrible about yourself, your art, your life. Some friends will make you feel like a loser because you have to almost beg them to meet up. Don't forget that the aim of this work is to improve your mental health and provide you with a support system that will help you when things get tough. If you don't think that someone will be there for you, it's time to take a big breath and cut them out of your life. It isn't a real connection if it makes you feel bad just thinking about it.

This, by the way, is also applicable to your family and romantic relationships. You don't have to suffer the presence of some people just because they are family. It is often heartbreaking and the cause of a lot of drama, but you should never keep someone in your life that makes you constantly feel bad, no matter who they are to you. It will probably make you feel guilty, but in the long run it will be healthier and easier.

I have had to seriously cut down the time I spend with two people in my family who are very toxic, to me and to everyone around them. I could not cut them out completely, but I at least manage to spend as little time as possible with them, without creating World War III in my family. It has made me much happier, even if I felt a bit guilty.

So, as you can see, this is not an easy thing to do, and sometimes you can't totally phase people out. But the quality of your relationships will directly influence the quality of your thoughts. And sometimes, no matter how awkward and difficult it is, you have to make a cut.

ROLE MODELS

Hope is a vital component in mental health: not only does it help people who are recovering from mental illness[23], it also plays a role in

---

[23] Acharya, Tanvi and Mark A Agius, "The importance of hope against other factors in the recovery of mental illness", *Psychiatria Danubina* (2017). Available online: https://www.semanticscholar.org/paper/The-importance-of-hope-against-other-factors-in-the-

the onset of these illnesses. Keeping hope alive is a very tricky thing for an artist because very often it takes years and years before success comes knocking at the door.

This is why having a few select people to look up to is crucial. Is there anyone in your field, famous or not, that you feel is the example you'd like to follow? Is there someone that you admire enough to want to dig deeper and understand what makes them tick?

It's not enough to just know that these people exist. To be able to use them as inspiration and build hope from their example, it's very important to know more about them, about how they think, and about how they work. It's much easier for you to try to reproduce small things that they do consistently, instead of pining after their success and wondering how they did it.

So, how do you learn more about your role models? Well, I'm an avid reader, and I love to read non-fiction books, so for me, the best way to learn about someone who intrigues me is to read a biography, if they have one. Or their Wikipedia page, as a start. One of my biggest role models in life is Jane Fonda, and I was lucky enough to be able to learn a lot about her life thanks to a podcast[24]. You can read interviews, blogs, even stories from people who met them.

If your role model has social media, it's also a good idea to follow them and see what they are up to on a daily basis. Science-fiction author Gareth L Powell explained a great method to keep tab on his role models in his book, *About Writing*[25]: he used Twitter lists to add all of his "teachers", as he calls them. It allowed him to see the tweets of a few selected individuals, and have a feel for what they are like.

Do you already have role models? Even one successful person will do, to inspire you and give you hope that you can succeed too. What do you know about them? How can their journey help you?

Acharya-Agius/273258cf5aa86562875fcfd2c9492cde5ae9c1ad (accessed 5 March 2020)

[24] *You Must Remember This* podcast: http://www.youmustrememberthispodcast.com/

[25] Powell, Gareth L, *About Writing*, Luna Press Publishing (2019). Available online: https://www.garethlpowell.com/

TECHNOLOGY

We are very fortunate to live in a time when technology can be a formidable ally to help us keep our mental health in check. I know that very often, technology is blamed for causing mental health issues, but I believe that, used wisely, it can be tremendously helpful.

For example, there are apps such as Headspace[26] that you can use to meditate and keep track of your progress. There are tools, such as Fitbit, that can gently push you to do more exercise and be more active. You can use your phone's calendar or reminders to help you manage your time, without having to stress about it.

I suffer from seasonal affective disorder, which means that, come winter, I feel sluggish and depressed because of the lack of light. I bought a special lamp designed to treat this, and I feel 100% better when I use it.

Some people use ASMR videos or programmes to treat their anxiety and/or sleep disorders, and find it more effective than any pill or medication. There are also very promising results[27] with therapies using video games, which can be used to treat a wide range of issues, in mental and general health.

There are so many apps and programmes and tools that are available now that could help you. I encourage you to research and test some of these solutions, as you might be surprised by the results.

FEELING ALIVE

Adulthood is so boring. Have you noticed that things get more and more muddled together as we age? Days, weeks, months, even years get mixed together into a giant ball of nothingness. When I was a child,

---

[26] Headspace: https://www.headspace.com/

[27] Kato, Pamela M, "Video Games in Health Care: Closing the Gap", *Review of General Psychology* (2010). Available online: https://journals.sagepub.com/doi/abs/10.1037/a0019441 (accessed 5 March 2020)

I firmly believed that my life would be exciting, that there would be a new adventure every day, but that's not how life works.

We need to work, pay the bills, do chores, commute, and a lot of things that are not inherently exciting because that's how life is. Unless you can afford not to work and have exciting adventures every day, that's probably how you feel too.

And quite honestly, this is a thought that really depresses me. The idea that there isn't much more, most days. That the excitement that I see publicised on TV or read about in books is just not everyday life for most people. Sometimes it feels like the child inside of me dies of boredom, and screams to give up everything and do something crazy.

So, from time to time, I allow my inner child to take charge. I purposefully introduce excitement in my life, in a controlled way, instead of letting myself explode one day because I've repressed this side of myself. A "non-controlled explosion", as I call it, can be damaging for your life, your relationships and your career. The idea here is to let off some of steam so that you don't feel like you are just working, working, working. It's basically a way to be happy now, instead of waiting for an hypothetical future that might not happen.

A few examples of the stuff that I do purely to feel alive and excited:

- On a day off work, I go to the nearest train station and take the first train to a city that I don't know. The unknown is exciting!
- I try a completely new activity, like fishing from a boat on holiday
- I take a different route to work, just because
- I do something that really scares me, like walking on a tall bridge that has a glass floor, even though I'm really afraid of heights
- I attend a meet up with people I've never met before, doing something I've never done before either
- I go to a hill or high place, to have a view on the entire city, and I write what I see
- I go to the nearest theatre or concert hall and buy a ticket to a show that I've never heard about, just to discover something new that I wouldn't have tried otherwise

There are many more ways to feel excited, but I think the common denominator to all of these is trying something new. Surprise yourself, make yourself less predictable.

This is particularly effective if, like me, you become anxious when life is too much of the same, when routine sets in and you feel completely trapped. And it doesn't need to cost a lot of money!

HOBBIES

As artists, we often consider our art as a hobby-that's-not-a-hobby. From me, writing was a hobby, and it has now become more than that. I think, to have a good life balance, that our art needs to be its special self, and therefore you need at least one real hobby.

Indeed, if your goal is to progress and perhaps one day make a living from your art, you will find yourself in a position where you might get stressed by your art, or not find it as enjoyable sometimes because you have a pressure to be productive.

For me, writing is still fun, but some days it also feels like pulling a tooth. I can have fun and write with no other purpose than enjoying it, but I find that the more I progress, the more everything I write is destined to help me accomplish my goal of becoming a successful author. That adds up to a hell of a lot of pressure!

So, I need something to do just because it's fun, with no other agenda. It's a way to find moments for myself, the same way I take breaks and pamper myself. It doesn't mean that your hobby can't be artistic, or have nothing to do with what you do for your art. But I think it's important to draw a line and make sure that your hobby is done "for the sake of it", instead of being "useful".

I paint figurines. I also am learning to paint my nails with patterns. I love cooking, and I'm decent at sewing. None of these are done to further my creative career. I do them because they are fun and fit me.

But in a world that is already so busy, between work and your art, how in the hell do you make time to have a hobby?

If you have read *The Part-Time Artist*, you know that I only achieve everything I say I do by using a weekly planner. I write all the elements of my week on a piece of paper, starting with work shifts, commute, meetings and things that I can't change. Then chores and obligations. Then I make sure I have writing sessions. And then, I make sure I have time for meeting friends, relaxing, exercising and hobbies. It's a game of Tetris, and some weeks I can't achieve the right balance, but I do my best to make sure I don't go crazy.

Making sure that you have some time for yourself, to do things that are completely not useful, is a great way to say to yourself, "I love you".

HEALTH CHECKS

Recently, I've been feeling extremely tired and morose, and I wasn't sure why. It started at the beginning of the year, and I put it down to quitting my job and getting used to working mostly from home, a new rhythm and some probable PTSD from the year and a half of abuse. I thought that it was all in my head, that maybe I was depressed or something.

Then, during the summer, I finally thought that perhaps it had nothing to do with any of this—that maybe it would be a good idea to go to the doctor to get a blood test, because I was developing new symptoms: I often felt lightheaded, nauseated, was gaining weight and feeling extremely tired even after a good night's sleep.

Low and behold, my symptoms had a physical health explanation: I discovered that my thyroid was not producing enough hormones. Anyone who's ever suffered from hypothyroidism will tell you, the level of fatigue is incredible. I've been taking hormone replacement pills for months now and it's day and night with how I felt before!

My story should serve as a cautionary tale. I know that a lot of people avoid going to the doctor for one reason or another. I know that often it is because doctors and blood tests are expensive. But think about the fact that you could be missing something that will dramatically change your quality of life. That, more than anything, is worth investigating. If you are lucky enough to be able to afford going to the doctor, I advise you to do a blood test at the very least every two years and see your doctor from time to time to check that everything is okay, not just when you are sick.

There might be some underlying reasons of why you feel how you feel. Don't dismiss biological causes, even if you've had mental health issues before that had nothing to do with your health. There are many factors that can make you feel depressed or anxious, such as vitamin deficiency or sleep apnea.

On the other hand, mental health issues can also cause biological problems. I suffer from psoriasis, which is directly associated with my anxiety. Therefore, when talking about treatment with a doctor, it's a good idea to disclose what you are struggling with in order to give them a full picture.

PROFESSIONAL HELP

Most people believe that they need to be at breaking point before being able to see a doctor or a therapist to help alleviate their problems.

I strongly believe that therapy can be as (if not more) effective as a preventive tool. In my opinion, it's better to do something about an existing problem before this problem becomes too much to handle or creates dangerous outcomes, such as suicidal thoughts or self-harm behaviours.

There's another reason why I always recommend people to research the possibilities of therapy around them, even if they don't necessarily think it's a pressing matter. In many countries around the world, access to therapy, doctors or mental health help is not simple. In the UK, where I live, it took around three months from my first assessment and diagnostic of General Anxiety Disorder, to my first therapy session. And I was amongst the lucky ones, as I had access to a programme that was championed by the mental health charity, Mind[28], and that a place was available fairly quickly. It doesn't always work this way. You might wait several months, sometimes over a year.

Obviously, doctors and therapists prioritise people who are in an emergency situation, but I would argue that it's best to be prepared and seek help when you are still able to wait, than have to wait when it is already very late.

Money is also a consideration in this case. When I went through Mind for therapy, I only paid £10 per session (around $12). It was very affordable, and I'm aware how lucky I was. In many countries, accessing therapy can be much more costly than that. Planning financially for it, again when you are not yet at the end of your rope, is the best course of action.

----

[28] Mental Health Charity Mind: https://www.mind.org.uk/

Don't wait until you are in crisis to research the possibilities of help. Trust me, by then you might not feel strong enough to go through all the hoops.

CHAPTER FIVE

CRISIS STRATEGIES

Times of Crisis

Sometimes, prevention is just not enough. Some events happen that can make your mental health worse. Sometimes, the illness wins and overwhelms you. Sometimes, it's just not your month or year.

Mental health is a tricky thing, and sometimes you can do everything right and still feel like crap. You can feel like you are achieving a lot, and then something derails you and precipitates you in a drowning pool. Or your circumstances might be too tough at the moment, and nothing you do works.

I've been there. I've tried to keep my head out of the water, but there came a time when it was not enough.

This chapter is not meant to make you feel worse, and it certainly doesn't mean that you should not apply the techniques that I've written about previously. The idea here is to plan what to do if you get in a situation where a crisis is inevitable.

Very much like we make plans in case of catastrophes and disasters, it's a good idea to have a plan in mind in case your mental health takes a turn for the worse. I'll also go over some mental health first aid that you can apply to yourself or to other people, the same way you would learn first aid to deal with injuries and wounds.

It's also best to do this now, while you feel good enough to do a little bit of research and you feel confident that you can do something about it. Don't wait until you feel so bad that you can't help yourself. Very much like the prevention techniques, this is best done, tested, rehearsed even, before the problem happens.

RECOGNISE THE CRISIS

First, let's define what a crisis is. What I mean by "crisis" is when you can't function anymore, when you can't achieve what you want because your mind is torturing you too much. It's when you can't perform at work, when you can't be happy at home, and when your life is spent dealing with terrible thoughts. Sometimes, a crisis means that you will lose sight of reality, with psychotic episodes such as hallucinations or paranoia.

For some people, a crisis episode might just last one day, and they feel better the next. It is often a sign to slow down, take care of themselves and probably seek help. But crisis episodes can last much longer. It can mean that you start having panic attacks every time you leave your house. It can mean that you can't get out of bed for days on end. Or it can mean that you have recurring suicidal thoughts and start thinking about making them real.

I think the best way to describe it is "feeling at a breaking point". Nothing seems to work anymore; nothing seems to appease you or make you feel better.

Recognising that you are at this point is vital to being able to do something about it. Are you the type of person who, like me, always assure everyone that you are fine? I used to think, "I'm fine, I'm fine, it will pass" every time I had a panic attack. I would not admit to myself that this was not fine and that I needed to act on it, or it would get worse.

That's the tricky thing with mental health. We often react too late because we have internalised the false notions of "drama queen" and "whining". We believe that it's not as bad as it feels because it's just in our heads. Or we completely hide what we're feeling from the people we love because we feel ashamed, weak or unworthy of their attention.

The first step is to recognise that it is *not* fine, and that you need to do something about it. Avoid convincing yourself that things will get better on their own because, when it comes to mental health crisis, it rarely does.

Crisis Buddies

In many cases, if you have reached a point where you feel in crisis, you might not be able to get out of there by yourself. It's a very difficult thing to accept, especially if you pride yourself on being strong and independent like I do.

I didn't want to ask for help. I told no one of my depressive feelings for the longest time—not even my best friends! It was such a shameful thing to admit. And, years later, when I had my first panic attack, I didn't tell anyone about that either. I suffered through it alone, and it was awful.

So I get it. We get so good at hiding our true feelings that it becomes a second identity. To the world around us, we present this facade of strength and fake happiness, while inside we are crumbling.

In my experience, sometimes it's easier to talk to a stranger than to your own family. When I felt very low, after coming back from Switzerland, the first person I spoke to was my doctor. She was not exactly a stranger, but she also didn't know me very well. It felt easier to unload onto her than my family or friends. I knew I would feel less judged if I spoke to her, instead of speaking to people who knew me.

I have never used services such as The Samaritans[29], but they were on my list of organisations to contact in case I started to feel worse. I know they are brilliant and help a lot of people. There are countless charities and organisations that specialise in different types of mental health crisis, and I think it's a good idea to start your own list.

Get your workbook, and fill out the list provided. Write down a few organisations that could be helpful in the future for you, as well as their contact details. Tip: if you are like me and *hate* speaking on the phone to someone, there are organisations that use online chats, emails or texts as well as phone lines. Think about what would be the easiest for you to do in a moment when everything feels overwhelming.

---

[29] The Samaritans website: https://www.samaritans.org/

On your list, try to also add "real-life people". People who you know you can confide in, who you will be able to talk to and who will be there for you. My partner is at the top of my list, and he was the one person who helped me the most when I had the worst of my panic attacks. We did not even live together at the time, but he managed to calm me down over the phone.

I know it will be difficult for you to select someone, and even more difficult to talk to them if the time comes, so another piece of advice I can give you that worked for me is to warn them in advance. Say to them, "I'm not feeling great, and one day I might need to talk and be heard." You can even set the rules with them, for example, that you don't want them to push you to do anything, just listen.

This list should be your first go-to when you recognise that you are in crisis.

STOPPING A PANIC ATTACK

Amongst the emergencies that I know well are panic attacks. Panic attacks are scary, and I'm lucky that I don't have them often anymore. The good thing about them is that they are almost never dangerous for you or your health, even if it feels like you are dying.

Weirdly, I never have a panic attack out of the blue. Some people do, but I always know when it's coming. It's usually on a day that has already been rotten and awful, when I've felt anxious from the beginning of the day, or for a few days already. I often slept badly and felt tired and in prime condition to let my anxiety take over.

Not everyone's symptoms are the same. I've had to deal with other people's panic attacks before as a first aider in theatre, and not two of them were the same. As a result, everyone's coping techniques are different. You could have physical symptoms such as chest pains that can be very frightening. You could feel out of breath, or suddenly feel like you need to breathe very quickly. Some people feel like they are going to be sick, with sweating and nausea, and sometimes throw up. I've met a woman whose muscles would go into full cramps for several long minutes. You could also cry uncontrollably and hyperventilate as a result.

Knowing that this is the case, it means that not all methods are going to work for you. I advise you to try different techniques and see what helps you calm down and helps you manage the symptoms. I have found that breathing exercises are what worked the best for me, along with having someone reassuring nearby or on the phone to soothe me. You might need to evacuate the negative and stressed energy first, so for some people, light exercise might work.

Using mindfulness or focus techniques are another method you can use: focusing on one object in the room, or training your mind to search for three objects of a certain colour, then do it again and again. It's called "grounding", and it really helps if your thoughts are completely unleashed, and you feel like you can't get out of your own head.

If your panic attack is caused by too much stimuli around you, closing your eyes is always a good idea. Using noise-cancelling headphones when possible is also a way to reduce the pressure on your over-stimulated brain.

It didn't work for me at all, but some people get really good results with essential oils and/or homeopathy. If it is at all possible, taking a shower with some nice smells might help you relax, and forces you to breathe more deeply. On the other end, you can also use things like an ice pack, or a hot water bottle to help you with chest pains or muscle pains. It also helps you grounding yourself though your sense of touch.

Repeating an inspiring thought or mantra is another small thing that can make a big difference. You can do it yourself, or have someone do it for you. A simple sentence, such as "it will be okay", repeated over and over, can act as a very soothing music to your brain. And talking about music, some deep relaxing songs can also help you.

Finally, if self-help doesn't improve your situation, professional help might be necessary. Talking therapies and medicines can be used to alleviate your symptoms. Certain types of antidepressants can be really useful in the treatment of your panic attacks, as well as some types of anti-epilepsy drugs and beta blockers.

Keep in mind that a panic attack rarely lasts longer than a few minutes. It's painful and difficult, and sometimes really scary, but if you are aware that it is going to pass eventually, it makes the experience easier.

Panic attacks are almost always a symptom of something bigger. In my case, it was how I realised that my anxiety was much deeper than a simple "worrying" personality. I see them as a blessing in disguise because it's the only way I understand that I need to deal with some feelings, slow down, assess and be kind to myself. It's my body's way of taking back control when I've pushed it too far. And I see the fact that they have slowed down in the past year as a good sign, meaning that I'm much better at dealing with my emotions than I used to be.

WHEN TO ASK FOR HELP

Asking for help is the hardest part of a mental health crisis. The first concern is: when to ask for help? In my experience, things don't degenerate suddenly for many people. Unless there is a pre-existing condition, it often takes months or years to go down the path of anxiety and depression. And so the question arises: why should I ask for help today when I'm barely worse than I was yesterday? Perhaps I feel a bit better, even if I know it's only a respite.

When I seeped slowly into depression, I could have gone like that for many more months without realising that I needed help to get out of it. But I was lucky, because one event made me realise that things were not fine and that I was drowning. It was my twenty-fifth birthday. Being twenty-five years old doesn't seem like such a big deal anymore (I'll be almost ten years older than that when this book comes out), but at the time, it was a very big deal. A quarter of a century. The first "check-point" of my twenties.

And by twenty-five, my twenties were not going well at all. I was unemployed, living in an old house with flatmates, having a really bad relationship with my parents, had failed at being a scientist and felt like I had no direction in my life whatsoever. For that birthday, the only thing I really wanted to do was go out to a club and get really really really drunk. But my friends, all being in a much more stable life than I was, didn't feel like it, and so we just had a dinner, and then they all left. Something like that shouldn't have bothered me that much, but that day I felt betrayed. I felt like a loser. I felt like I couldn't even get this one little thing out of my life.

It was a Friday, and I didn't leave my bed until the Sunday night of that weekend. I am not a crier, but that weekend I cried so much that my face was sore. And I want to be very clear: I did not cry because of my friends. I cried because I realised how much of a farce my life was. How depressed I had been. How much hope I had put in this small get-together with my friends, as if it would somehow cure everything that had gone wrong in my life up to this point.

It was not pretty. I'm not proud of that weekend. But at the same time, I'm incredibly grateful that it happened, because that Sunday evening I came to the conclusion that I needed help. That if I didn't get help, right then, right now, it would be too late. So the following Monday morning, I made two bookings: I booked an appointment with a psychotherapist in my area, and I booked three months worth of Krav Maga (a combat sport) lessons. The therapy is self-explanatory, and the idea of the sport was that I felt so powerless and so angry at the same time that I knew I needed an way to let all of these feelings out. This was the first step to getting better.

I feel like many people ask for help after an experience like mine. Very often, it's one thing, that can be very small, that makes them decide "that's it, I need help". But there's also a danger with this line of thought: that perhaps you'll wait for a "sign" and risk going deeper into your problems. Trust me, the longer you wait, the harder it is.

If anything, this book can be your sign. If you feel in crisis, if you feel like you keep going down and there's no respite, nothing ever makes it better, then the time to ask for help is *now*.

How to Ask for Help

Next to "when", "how" is also very tricky. There's a fear, almost primal, that might tell you that if you ask for help, you'll be shunned by the people around you. You'll be mocked, made to feel worse or even not trusted. I have it, we all have it. Which is why asking for help is so hard! This fear is so deeply ingrained in most of us that, if someone shows concern about us, we might even lie and send them away.

So in this section, I want to talk about "low risk" ways of asking for help, where it's easier and where you have less risk of being rejected.

As I said in the "crisis buddies" section, if you have made a list before you reach crisis, it is time to use it. It's probably the path of least resistance because you have already done your research, and potentially already talked to some people on the list about the fact that you might need help someday.

But if you are in crisis right now and you haven't had time to make a buddy list yet, here are some options:

- Your doctor – as I said earlier, doctors tend to be better trained in mental health now than they were ten years ago. Health professionals, including nurses and even pharmacists, now have to go through mental health trainings in many countries. I've found that, at least in the UK, doctors will be better informed and will at least be able to direct you to the best person or service depending on your problem. Of course, I know that in many places it's difficult to see a doctor, because it's too expensive or because they are swamped and only treat emergencies. But if you are lucky enough to be in a position to see a GP, it is a good first dip into trying to get some help.
- Accidents & Emergencies – alternatively, if you are in danger of harming yourself, you can go directly to your nearest emergency service. A lot of hospitals nowadays have a psychiatric service or access to one, and specialised people that can help you if you experience dissociation with reality, suicidal or self-harming episodes. Even if your local hospital is small, they will have the contacts needed to help you.
- An organisation or charity specialising in mental health – I have mentioned the Samaritans and Mind before, but there are hundreds of organisations and charities that will have different

specialities and focuses. They often make a point of being easy to contact, and to reply as quickly as possible. For some, you can call, for some you can email, or even self-refer yourself to their services.

- Drop-in groups or sessions – we probably all have seen a rendition of an Alcoholics' Anonymous group meeting in a film or a TV series. Did you know that there are similar group activities for a lot of other problems? In my area, there is a mental health café for example, where you can drop in and chat with people, without having to make a booking or appointment. Support groups and chat sessions are very helpful because you don't have to worry about booking, which can really help when you already feel too overwhelmed to function.
- Community services – sometimes, you might feel like you need help in a specific area before you can get help with your mental health. For example, you might need help with dealing with debt, facing an abusive relationship, or even need legal help. These services are low-risk because they don't tackle your mental health issues directly, but help you improve and alleviate some of the surrounding problems that make you feel worse.
- Something unrelated but that you know will make you feel better – whether it's starting a sport, like I did, or doing other types of activities, it's still asking for help, even if you don't specify why you want to participate. When I had my first session of Krav Maga, I didn't say that I needed it for my mental health, but I said that I felt weak and lost, and needed help. And it's exactly what I got.

I know that this might still feel overwhelming and difficult, which is why I'm going to give you the one piece advice that helped me the most: ONE THING AT A TIME

There's so much pressure on you right now that you might feel like you will make a mistake, not select the best therapist, the best option, not do it anonymously enough or not go to all meetings. Now, take a deep breath, and just do one thing. Just one. Like booking an appointment with your regular doctor. Boom. Done. You've done it for today. Tomorrow, you'll do something else.

TREATMENTS

Depending on your issues, your past and the severity of the crisis, different courses of action can be taken. One of the key objectives of people who will help you is to first stop the crisis. For example, if you have a psychotic episode, they will make sure to treat that first, as it is an emergency, particularly if you are in danger of harming yourself or others. Then the focus will move to treating the underlying problem, such as depression, anxiety or other illnesses. You might get a diagnostic at this point, or they might search for other reasons that could explain your symptoms too.

Sometimes, medication might bring temporary or long-term relief, depending on what has been found. I have never taken chemical antidepressants, but I was advised by my doctor to take St John's Wort, which is a natural solution for mood disorders.

Usually—and especially if you are treated by a psychotherapist—there will be a plan for what is going to happen: therapy sessions, medication, group sessions and/or lifestyle changes.

Therapy can be scary. There is still a terrible stigma against people who see a therapist. You might wonder: what is therapy exactly? How does it work? What do we talk about? Am I going to lie on a sofa while the therapist doodles? We all have seen stereotypical scenes of therapy in films or TV series, but in my experience, the real thing is pretty different.

I've been through different types of therapies, with different types of practitioners. The first was with a gynaecologist who doubled as a therapist for sexual disorders. Her style was very direct, asking questions and giving me exercises to do at home to help with my problems. The second therapist I saw was a psychologist who helped me through my depression. I sat in front of her desk and most of the sessions were a chat between us about things that I had on my mind. I had a couple of assignments to do, but mostly the work was done with her, trying to figure out how I could get out of the depression.

Years later, I did a CBT-based therapy with an NHS-certified therapist for my self-esteem problems. This one was very different and consisted of mainly doing assignments at home, and reporting my progress to the therapist. We would talk about events that happened in the past week, how I perceived them and how I reacted to them. I briefly followed up this work with another NHS-certified "talking" therapy, where the therapist was mostly silent, never asked questions and let me talk. I hated that one! Finally, the last one that I did for my anxiety last year was another where the therapist asked questions and suggested other interpretations to my thoughts. They taught me how to meditate, how to ground myself and other tricks that I've discussed in this book.

As you can see, there isn't just one type of experience with therapy, and it's up to you to decide what you would feel most comfortable with. I hate the idea of group therapy, but it helps some people tremendously.

Finally, I also would like to mention that you don't necessarily need a "therapist" in the conventional sense. A lot of people find benefits in alternative therapies, with other types of professionals. Acupuncture, EFT, herbal medicine, energy healing—there are dozens of things to try. I would just recommend caution when trying out these other solutions, as there are far fewer safeguards for these therapies than there is in psychotherapy, and therefore much more charlatans Do your research before spending huge amounts of money!

RECOVERY

You can recover from a crisis. I know that it might seem impossible, but I'm here to tell you that it's absolutely possible.

Recovery is the time to concentrate on yourself and make sure you follow all the recommendations that you get. Going through a crisis is difficult, and it's hard to get out of it for good. My biggest fear after my depression was to go back into it at some point. Quite frankly, years later, this is still a big fear of mine. And it's even more scary when you look at the statistics around relapses.

However, it doesn't need to be all doom and gloom. When you go through something like a nervous breakdown, a depression or a psychotic episode, you'll have the opportunity to make changes that might have seemed impossible before. While recovering from my depression, I had the courage to sort things out with my family and establish proper limits, something that I had never been able to do before. My motto was "never again". It allowed me to make the changes necessary in my life. A crisis episode is often a sign that you need to change something, and therefore don't hesitate to take it as an opportunity to make changes in your life.

Recovering doesn't mean that you'll be "cured". You might still need to take antidepressants or other types of medication for a long time. You might need to continue therapy on a less intense rhythm. Recovery means that you are able to continue your life after the crisis, and live it to the fullest extent possible. Whether that means that you can manage your symptoms and can go back to work or your family life, or that you have found a new purpose for yourself, that's up to you to decide.

When I recovered from depression, the most important component to my journey was to get hope back. I had felt hopeless for so many months, convinced that things would never get better, that daring to hope again was the best sign that I was recovering. I threw myself into a new career, with new challenges and new people, and managed to get rid, little by little, of my depressive symptoms.

However, it is a misconception that things will go back to "normal" after recovery. My "normal" changed after every crisis. It is not a bad thing—on the contrary, those changes were badly needed, such as changing job, changing my entourage and changing the country I lived in.

But the change is not just external. Mental illness made me a different person. I am much more compassionate and attentive to the people around me now. I feel like I'm much less of a "know it all", and I understand that other people's experiences might be different than mine. I'm also quicker at identifying how I feel and listening to my "gut feelings", which I didn't do before.

Recovery is a process. It takes time and patience. But it happens.

CHAPTER SIX
KEEP CREATING

LONG-LASTING ARTIST

Being an artist is incredibly difficult in the long run. Everyone can be creative for a few weeks or months, but when success doesn't knock at the door, how can we continue to perform?

This is probably one of the biggest challenges you will face in your artistic life. In my previous book, I wrote about the fact that circumstances (like money, family, day job) might force you to quit and you would have to be organised enough and determined enough to continue your art. But I think that the biggest reason many people quit is internal.

How do you keep going when your mind is relentlessly harassing you and making you feel miserable? How do you keep yourself motivated when you are battling depression? How do you seize opportunities when the simple idea of networking gives you an anxiety attack?

This section is all about tips and tricks that I have developed over the years to continue writing, despite everything but especially despite myself.

Keep Inspiration Alive

One of the key components of being an artist is the inspiration we get about projects and things that we do. Unfortunately, inspiration can be threatened when we feel bad about ourselves.

Do you feel like you haven't had a good idea in a long time? It has happened to me. Sometimes, it's because I've finished a big project and I feel completely empty. Sometimes, it's because every idea is immediately shot down by my inner saboteur. It's very difficult to envisage a big enterprise when everything inside yourself tells you that you will fail.

But here again, I have tips to help you feel inspired more often, and protect these ideas when your brain is not ready to apply them.

The first thing that you should do on a daily basis is to make sure you get enough of what I call "inputs of creativity", meaning making sure that you read, watch or listen to enough artistic outputs that can inspire you on a regular basis. We often get so focused on a project that we let this very important medium of inspiration dry out. We stop discovering new genres, books, bands, artists and therefore we don't get enough new ideas.

I am guilty of not doing this enough. My time is limited, and therefore when it comes to watching TV, for example, I only invest time in safe bets, stuff I've watched before or stuff I'm sure I will like. The problem is that I lose the opportunity to see things that will surprise me and give me totally different ideas. I also am guilty of reading books of the same genre, and I always listen to the same music.

This is something I'm trying to be better at, because when I make the effort to discover new things, I always have lots of new ideas for my books and characters, for new projects for my business or I just feel more motivated.

Another very important activity to do is to find a way to record all your ideas, inspirations and things you find interesting. As a writer, I'm biased towards writing down all of my ideas in a notebook because it helps me figure out which are interesting and which ones I should keep there and wait to see if they can be applied to something further down the line. But you might prefer leaving voice messages to yourself, typing notes in a Word document, or even creating a Pinterest board.

The idea is to record everything before your inner saboteur has a chance to convince you that it's not a good idea. And yes, some of these might not be good ideas, but at least you have them gathered somewhere, and they can be useful in the future!

The third way you can jog your inspiration is to complete creative exercises that don't matter, by which I mean creating things that involve your imagination, your talents and your creativity, but that are never going to leave your house. One of the most stifling components of inspiration is the fear of being judged. When I write a book, I always imagine the feedback I will get from readers, the comments, the reviews, and it makes me very fearful. I think I probably don't explore and try out new things as much in my books because I know that they will be read at some point, and that scares me. I don't dare to get off the beaten track as much, for fear of judgment.

So, I make a point to also write pieces that will never be read by anyone else. These that are purely there for my own enjoyment, for trying out new things. It allows me to try much more, and sometimes some of these ideas make it into a future project, but most of it is just there to keep me alert.

So, let's think about it together. Which one of these three techniques do you think will be the most beneficial? What can you apply right here, right now? Which ones are you guilty of never doing? And why?

REINVENT YOURSELF

A secret that many long-lasting artists share is that they don't do the same thing throughout their career. They understand that, as people, we evolve all throughout our lives, and therefore need to allow our art to evolve too.

Even "classical" artists had various periods in their work. Take Pablo Picasso. He had a "blue" period, a "rose" period, a "cubism" period (for which he's best known) and so on, following the art trends of his time. He allowed himself to be inspired by different things, gave up stuff that had worked for him at one time but didn't work anymore, followed ideas and muses.

In a totally different field, one of my biggest role models is Jane Fonda. She's a particularly interesting artist to follow because almost every decade of her life saw a reinvention of herself. She was the "babe" in films such as Barbarella, before completely changing herself into a political activist, then changing again into a fitness guru, living many lives in one. It doesn't mean that she completely rejected every previous iteration of herself, but that she followed her heart into a new venture, understanding that life is too short to lock yourself into one identity and one persona.

I've been a writer for twenty years, but I haven't been the same writer for all those years. I went from a teenager experimenting with different styles, to an acclaimed fanfiction author, to writing science-fiction, to non-fiction currently. I follow where my inspiration leads me because I understand that if I don't keep moving, my soul will not continue to be enriched.

What does this mean for you? It means that you don't need to be one thing for the rest of your life. If you feel that somehow your art doesn't bring you as much joy as it used to, it might be a sign that you need to explore a different avenue. It also means that you shouldn't be scared to do something completely different than what you've done before.

I know there's a lot of pressure for you to continue in one way. I was pushed by the people who read my fanfiction to continue and write another one after I finished my longest, "Eternal Snow". I was tempted, and I actually wrote three-quarters of another fanfiction, but I realised that the time for fanfiction was gone for me. It didn't bring me as much joy, as much fulfilment as it once did. I had to find the next thing in my artistic life.

Have you already had different periods in your artistic life? Or perhaps you feel like your current period is coming to an end and you don't know what comes next?

It can be difficult to give up a part of our identity to go to something completely new, so let me give you a few pointers:

- What makes you passionate right now? What can you spend time researching, reading about, watching videos or documentaries?
- How do you feel about your previous work? Would you do something similar again? If not, why not?

- Do you feel pressured to keep on going?

Allowing yourself to go in different directions can be very freeing because then, if you feel like quitting, it might just mean quitting what you are doing right now, not necessarily quitting being an artist altogether. You can totally be a singer, then decide you want to branch into fashion or painting. There's nothing that prevents you from doing it, apart the judgment of other people.

HAVE FUN

I find that now that I'm well into my thirties, I need to remind myself constantly that I write in part because it's fun. It's fun to invent new worlds and create the characters that live in it. It's fun to talk about my life and the lessons I've learned along the way. It's fun to publish a book, go to conferences and talk to other artists.

However, day to day life is often boring. Routine kills the fun, and therefore we don't associate art and fun anymore. This is why I believe it's highly important to remind ourselves of the fun of it all, and to take our art much less seriously. There need to be times when you remember the joy that you have doing what you do.

Remind yourself of the first time you wrote a chapter, climbed on stage, played an instrument, grabbed a paintbrush or got your hands on a camera. The pure, childish joy that you felt then has probably faded now, but that doesn't mean that it has completely disappeared. You can call back to it and feel it again if you try hard and often enough.

I have a little trick that I do on a regular basis: I try to make myself laugh with something that I write. It's often the most ridiculous thing in the world, but it really helps remind myself that this is not serious at all. That I can have fun.

It is especially necessary when you are working on a demanding project, perhaps even something depressing. I remember a discussion I had with a theatre manager who told me that the performers working on a particular show were having a really hard time with their mental health because the show was so dark and talked about horrific events. This is when it's important to remind yourself that your art can also be light, fun and breezy from time to time. It doesn't matter if what you do most of the time is dark and sad—these little pockets of "fun" can be just yours.

After I finished drafting this book, which took a lot of mental fortitude to complete, I am intending to write something that is going to be completely crazy fun and that I will probably never publish, just because I need to have a little bit of an easy time before I start editing.

If you are stuck on a long project that is hard on your morale, or if you just have had a tough month or year, consider doing something purely for the fun of it. Remind yourself of what you once felt, and chase that feeling now.

At the end of the day, we are artists. We don't solve war, famine or diseases. We are allowed to have fun. Remember that.

CONCLUSION

This is the end of our journey together, and I hope that you have enjoyed the time we have spent discussing mental health and artistry.

I really believe that each of us can improve our mood and mental health by applying some of these strategies over and over again. Things don't get better overnight, and sometimes you need to go through a crisis to decide on some heavy changes. But at the end of the day, I feel like we can all make better decisions that will make our minds healthier, the same way we can train and diet to improve our body's health.

I hope that this book has also helped you realise that you are not alone in your struggles. I've tried to be as open and transparent as possible, even if it is still difficult for me to do so. I feel exposed, and sometimes ashamed, but I also feel freer. I sincerely hope that it has shown you that it is okay to discuss mental health problems because if nobody shares their experience, we can't find solutions.

Don't hesitate to share your ideas, experiences or struggles with me. You can reach me on my website:

theparttimeartist.com

By email:

info@theparttimeartist.com

Or on social media:

@CelineTerranova (Twitter, Instagram)

And finally:

Being an independent author means that I rely on your reviews to get this book noticed by other potential readers. I would really appreciate it if you took the time to post a review on your favourite retailer website (Amazon, Kobo, B&N, etc.) and on Goodreads.

Feel free to publicise it on social media, and don't hesitate to tag me into your post. If you think that my book helped you on your journey, please let others know.

ACKNOWLEDGEMENTS

This book was particularly challenging to write, and therefore I would like to thank the people who made it easier every step of the way:

Eirik Knutsvik, for being my rock, my partner and my best friend. This book would not have existed without you.

My family and my friends, in Belgium and in the UK. Your support is invaluable to me.

My editor, Vicky Brewster, my illustrator, Juan Carlos Porcel and my cover artist Angie Alaya. Your hard work and inputs have made this book a hundred times better.

The Part-Time Artist family, readers and followers, all around the world. I feel extremely lucky to have met you this year, and I am looking forward to know you all better.

www.ingramcontent.com/pod-product-compliance
Lightning Source LLC
Chambersburg PA
CBHW070714250726
48662CB00001B/411